Text by Albert R. Leventhal

WAR

Picture Research by Del Byrne

Hamlyn | London • New York • Sydney • Toronto

Editor-in-Chief: Jerry Mason
Editor: Adolph Suehsdorf
Art Director: Albert Squillace
Associate Editor: Moira Duggan
Associate Editor: Barbara Hoffbeck
Associate Editor: Jean Walker
Art Associate: Mark Liebergall
Art Associate: David Namias
Art Production: Doris Mullane

Published in the UK in 1973 by
The Hamlyn Publishing Group Limited
London • New York • Sydney • Toronto
Astronaut House, Feltham, Middlesex, England

ISBN 0 600 39304 6

Printed in Italy by
Arnoldo Mondadori Editore, Verona

"But what good came of it at last?"
Quoth Little Peterkin.
"Why that I cannot tell," said he;
"But 'twas a famous victory."

Robert Southey, *The Battle of Blenheim*

Contents:

In this bewildering century tens of millions of human beings have gone to their death in war or a by-product of war—on a thousand battlefields, in bombed cities, jungles, or concentration camps. A vast percentage of the world's population has never known a month or a day when war, or the threat of war, did not exist.

In capsulizing some of the conflicts that are the legacy of our time, it is almost impossible for the conscientious historian to recapture the misery and horror that accompanied the roar of battle. No matter how hard he tries, old place names and old catch phrases take on fresh excitement and sound almost glamorous as the writer attempts to communicate the awful reality of a distant hour: Pickett's Charge, the Taxis of the Marne, Stalingrad, Iwo Jima. The heart beats just a bit faster at the very bigness of the moment, and the headless bodies and scraps of human flesh clinging to crumbling wars tend to be forgotten. Figures and statistics become meaningless and the reader takes in without blinking an eye a sentence that tells him 60,000 human beings lost their lives in a single day in the muddy hell of the Somme, or twice that number in a few seconds at Hiroshima.

A true detestation of war comes most forcefully to those who have seen its face: to the men who did the killing; to those who survived Auschwitz; to those whose faces and bodies, like a monstrous jigsaw puzzle, were put together again after Nagasaki; to those who visit veterans' hospitals to joke with youngsters who lost genitals, intestines, and legs along a nameless path or in a nameless rice paddy.

The camera's eye, which avoids generalities and freezes in time the ugly moment, conveys far better than words the dirt and insanity of the battleground. And so, out of tens of thousands of war pictures, the editors have chosen those they regard as coming closest to the truth, to the *way it really was.* Nearly all of them were taken by photographers who shared the battle, committing the breathless moment to film.

This volume also demonstrates how the acceleration of technological aptitudes has changed the face of war in the past century and a quarter. Under the pressures of battle, medicine and antisepsis have taken enormous strides forward; regrettably, the power to cure has not been able to keep pace with the power to kill. Today, most soldiers are reasonably well paid and supplied with assorted creature comforts behind the lines; in earlier times they were obliged to forage for loot. In our era, most big wars have arisen because of conflicting ideologies. In earlier times, with some notable exceptions, they were fought because one's neighbor was weaker or had richer grazing land or owned an excess of worldly goods. Finally, the wars of the past brought enemies face to face. In World War II opposing fleets were destroyed without sighting one another, and today we have the capacity to annihilate an enemy who is halfway around the world.

In ancient times the *Rota Fortunae,* or wheel of fortune, stressed the cyclical nature of human behavior: from peace wealth, from wealth pride, from pride war, from war poverty, from poverty humility, from humility peace. Today, with war endemic around the globe, this concept has slight relevance. In this book, for example, some fourteen conflicts are briefly summarized or mentioned. During the same period three or four times that number of wars were fought on bloody battlefields in Asia, Africa, Europe, and the two Americas. What happened in Biafra and Pakistan, South Africa and Afghanistan, had little or nothing to do with pride or humility, and a great deal to do with the drive to dominate.

Other clichés of the past are equally suspect. The idea that "There never was a good war or a bad peace" is particularly nonsensical. The settlement achieved at Versailles in 1918, like many others, made future conflict inevitable. As to good wars, that remains controversial but some were distinctly better than others. However much one may despise or fear Communism, there is no doubt that the Russian and Chinese revolutions and civil wars left the majority of human beings living in those areas healthier, happier, and in more hopeful circumstances. Equally, the war against Hitler and the Japanese may not have been good, but it almost certainly was necessary if hundreds of millions of people were not to be enslaved by ruthless Fascist dictatorship.

"Wars never settle anything" is another questionable proposition. America's Indian Wars, which are not mentioned in these pages because they were closer to massacres than wars, decisively settled, for all time, the future role of the original inhabitants of the land. The American Civil War insured that the United States would remain one nation indivisible for a long time to come, and the Russian Revolution made the return of absolute monarchy a dubious proposition, to say the least.

But what of the future? Are wars inevitable and are they, as some philosophers and historians contend, the highest expression of man? Listen, for a moment, to Heinrich von Treitschke: "That war should ever be banished from the world is a hope not only absurd, but profoundly immoral. It would involve the atrophy of many of the essential and sublime forces of the human soul. . . . A people which becomes attached to the chimerical hope of perpetual peace finishes irremediably by decaying in its proud isolation."

Even though one may dismiss Treitschke and scores of similar thinkers who have preached the virtues of war over the centuries as lunatics or fanatics, there is little doubt that more wars of a traditional nature will be fought. Man is too contentious, hatreds are too deep, poverty is too grinding in many parts of the world for us to think otherwise. This conclusion, however, does not necessarily imply that mankind will achieve the ultimate in warfare—extermination of all life on earth. Man has the capacity already, and in the future only minor technical advances can be made in the weapons of destruction. Thus, as Arnold Toynbee has pointed out, the question of survival or extinction must be decided on a psychological level, on the battleground of the human mind.

One possible way in which mankind can save itself from self-destruction, Dr. Toynbee contends, is by achieving a synthesis between widely contrasting civilizations or lifestyles. One such synthesis, says Toynbee, might be "a felicitous mixture of modern western dynamism with traditional Chinese stability." While the odds against such a synthesis or merger of contrasting civilizations are great, it may, in the long run, be the only way.

The skeptical reader may dismiss the Toynbee argument as visionary, but what are the other alternatives to Armageddon? Leagues of nations, World Courts, and today's U.N. have proved to be frail reeds. It is unlikely that they will prove more effective in the foreseeable future. Equally remote is the possibility that one superpower, like Rome or the British Empire in the past, will emerge to enforce an uneasy peace. In the years ahead, it may be that the world's existing superpowers—Russia, China, and the United States—will manage to reconcile their differences and keep a lid on the bubbling nuclear cauldron. But if this does not work, there is one last alternative: the hope that raw fear and the knowledge of certain and instant retaliation will prevent mankind from pressing the button to start an atomic war.

Nothing, alas, in man's long history indicates that fear has ever proved to be a workable deterrent. Nations have always rationalized the risks of war and concluded that they had found a viable way of killing without getting killed. This pattern will almost certainly persist in the future, and the race of man will be obliged to rely on something stronger than fear if it chooses to persist on this planet.

CRIMEAN WA

Only once in the hundred years between the Battle of Waterloo and the Battle of Mons did British troops fight on the continent of Europe—and then in a conflict which fully lived up to Barbara Tuchman's classic maxim: "War is the unfolding of miscalculations."

In the middle of the nineteenth century, Great Britain, proud, prosperous, and smug, watched with growing concern as the guns of the new Russian naval base at Sevastopol, at the top of the Black Sea, pointed in the direction of Constantinople. If the Sick Man of Europe, as Tsar Nicholas I had christened the sprawling and decayed Turkish empire, should suddenly expire, Constantinople would go with it and Russia would impose a clear and constant threat to British control of the Mediterranean. At least that was the opinion of the foreign minister, Lord Palmerston, whose detestation of Russian autocracy was equaled only by his opposition to democratic reform in his native England. For her part, Queen Victoria disliked and distrusted the bellicose Palmerston and sputtered helplessly when Old Pam, greatly loved by the British middle classes, went directly to the people and the popular press with his vendetta against the Russians. The average Britisher shared this distaste for the Tsar's regime, and France, for reasons of her own, opposed Russia, too.

The Church of the Nativity in Bethlehem was the immediate cause of the war. Bethlehem was Turkish territory and the church marked the site of the stable where Jesus had been born. Russian Orthodox monks wanted to place a star atop the church, but Roman Catholic monks objected. Ironically, a battle over the star ended in the death of several Orthodox monks. France took the Roman Catholic side, and Nicholas angrily charged that Turkish police had deliberately permitted the priests' murder. In 1853 Russia and Turkey went to war.

The Russian fleet annihilated the feeble Turkish navy, and angry British crowds responded by tramping through the streets of London. The British press, which had been violently anti-Russian from the outset, beat war drums, and virulent war fever seized a new generation of British youth which had read about the Napoleonic wars but not experienced them. The thin red line at Waterloo was mistily recalled. So was Nelson, expiring in a heroic spasm at Trafalgar. National pride hit an all-time high when in 1854 the Queen's war message was read in the House of Commons. A few dissenting voices were raised, but ignored. The idiocy of the entire affair can be summed in a sentence from Cecil Woodham-Smith's brilliant book, *The Reason Why:* "Mr. Disraeli's explanation did not seem much more satisfactory: he remarked that he thought we were going to war to prevent the Emperor of All the Russias from protecting the Christian subjects of the Emperor of Turkey." Napoleon III, using the same sort of logic, hastened to join the fray.

The miscalculations that led to the war were equaled only by the manner in which it was mismanaged. Nicholas's army, the apple of his eye, proved a sad disappointment. Its equipment was faulty, its tactics cumbersome, its transport hopeless. Before long, the Tsar's visage become "unrecognizable, his face had a greenish pallor, his profile had lengthened and his eyes had a fixed expression." In 1855 he sickened and died, leaving Alexander II to continue the struggle.

The allied side was marked by truly massive incompetence, bumbling direction by the High Command combined with breakdowns and failures by the commissariat. British soldiers starved and died six miles from Balaclava, where the fleet rode at anchor with provisions piled up between decks. The British tradition of muddling through resulted in men going into battle carrying the same Brown Bess muskets Wellington's troops had used against Napoleon. Cholera and dysentery took a shocking toll, and Florence Nightingale later said that at least 16,000 lives were lost through hopelessly bad administration. Ms. Nightingale, the war's only true hero, succeeded in cutting the death rate at Scutari Hospital in half, but unfortunately the sphere of her activities was limited.

In the spring of 1854 the allied troops landed at the Balkan town of Varna on the theory that Nicholas would make his war in the Danube basin. It was another mistake, for the only enemies encountered were disease, devastating heat, and lack of food, water, and medical supplies. With no help from her allies, the Turks drove off the Russians, who meekly retreated to their homeland.

A massive amphibious landing on the Crimean Peninsula, thirty miles north of Sevastopol, came next. Four days after it was completed the British and French made a

Preceding pages: British siege mortars, probably at Sevastopol, 1855.

headlong assault on the Russian positions near the banks of the Alma River. Prince Menshikov, the Tsar's commander, had his men dug in on heights overlooking the swiftly flowing river, and was so convinced that his position could not be assaulted that he invited some thirty young ladies to a picnic lunch on the summit to witness the enemy's destruction.

It was yet another boner. The French found a road up the steep cliffs, and the British, so overcome with thirst that they paused to drink as they struggled across the river amid a hailstorm of shot and shell, clambered up the slopes, assaulted, and took the great redoubt, the key to the Russian defenses. More blunders followed, the redoubt changed hands, and once more a heroic British charge won the day. By evening the Russians were streaming back toward Sevastopol.

If the allies had moved quickly they probably could have taken the fortress within a few days. They didn't, and so gave the Russians a chance to build up their defenses and withstand a unique siege in which the defenders outnumbered and were far better supplied than the assailants.

In the weeks that followed there came the Battle of Balaclava, where a foul-up of orders resulted in the death ride of the Light Brigade. Six hundred cavalrymen charged headlong into the entire Russian army. Fewer than 200 returned. Less than two weeks later it was the Russians' turn. An overwhelming mass of the Tsar's men went on the offensive but were repulsed, with huge losses, in the Battle of Inkerman.

Late in 1855, ten months after Inkerman, Sevastopol fell, and Tsar Alexander welcomed peace feelers. Discontent was rising in St. Petersburg, where the war had become increasingly unpopular. There were shocking tales in circulation of corruption among army commanders, rifles that wouldn't fire, and breakdowns in supply. As for the British and French, the glamour waned while cholera raged. Both sides had little difficulty in arranging the peace terms that were signed in Paris early the following spring. The provisions of the Treaty of Paris were almost as meaningless as the war itself. Every clause in it was remarkably short-lived.

The Crimean War, however, did have several significant results. It marked the first collaboration between France and England since the Crusades, a relationship that eventually led to the pre-World War I entente. It was the first conflict in which the virtues of sanitation and the need for nursing care became evident. Finally, it strengthened Britain's desire to avoid battle on Continental soil.

Above: Encampment of British
4th Light Dragoons on plains above Balaclava
looked neat and tidy, but wasn't. Men of the 4th
were among those soon to make fatal charge into Russian
batteries. Opposite: Batman attends
to creature comforts of British officer.

Cossack Bay, Balaclava's inadequate harbor. Within a few days after the British fleet had anchored, the water was crusted with refuse and a foul smell blanketed the entire area.

17

Above: Ismail Pasha commanded Turkish
troops so detested by British. Left: Winter
clothing was issued to men of 47th Regiment, but
was in short supply for other units.
Opposite: A 19th-century British officer
in full flower: Capt. Francis Baring of the
Fusilier Guards, a quartermaster
assigned to the Light Brigade.

Photographer Roger Fenton, the first to report war with a camera, called this picture "The Valley of the Shadow of Death." Actually, it was a harmless gully near Sevastopol, cluttered with Russian shot that had missed the target.

AMERICAN CIVIL

725

TIMOTHY H. O'SULLIVAN

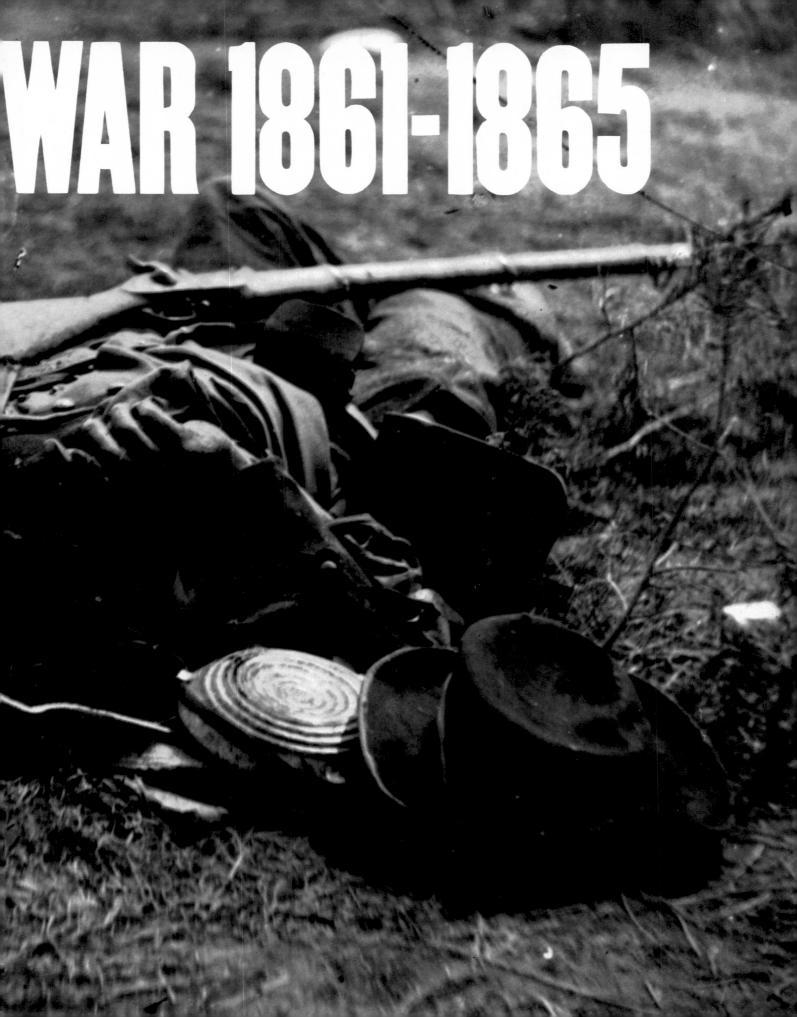

WAR 1861-1865

For thirty years before the guns spoke at Fort Sumter in the spring of 1861, an increasingly vituperative debate had been going on between the people who lived in the northern areas of the adolescent United States of America and their brethren who lived south of an imaginary barrier called the Mason-Dixon line.

On the surface the argument had to do with a peculiar institution—the selling of black men and black women to whites, as one sold hogs, cattle, or furniture. In reality, the issues at stake were more basic. The causes of the Civil War were economic: to determine whether a farming society could live alongside one that was becoming increasingly urbanized and industrialized. The causes were political as well: to decide whether a centralized government in Washington had the power to tell an individual, or the state in which he lived, how to regulate his life or his state's policies. In broader terms, once a state had joined a Federal union, did it have the right to withdraw from that union if it was dissatisfied with the manner in which the federation was being run?

In 1860 the six-year-old Republican party—an amalgam of former political parties that had drifted into obscurity, and Abolitionists who detested the traffic in black bodies—nominated an Illinois lawyer named Abraham Lincoln for the presidency. The platform of the party made no mention of slavery. Its slogan was "Vote Yourself A Farm."

Lincoln himself was equivocal on the subject of slavery but determined to preserve the Union. Two years earlier, campaigning against Stephen Douglas for a senatorial post from Illinois, he had preached equality of the races in Chicago but in the southern part of the state he said, "I am not, nor ever have been in favor of bringing about in any way the social and political equality of the black and white races. . . . I, as much as any other man, am in favor of the superior position being assigned to the white man."

With opposition to him divided, Lincoln was elected President with just forty percent of the vote. But in the months before he took office, South Carolina seceded from the Union and was soon followed by five sister states. The Confederate States of America, with Jefferson Davis as President, became a reality, and Texas soon became its seventh member.

The weeks dragged by as both sides waited to see what would happen in key border states lying between the North and the South. In early April, Lincoln made his first move, deciding to resupply Sumter in Charleston harbor, one of the few Federal forts in the South that had not been seized by the seceding states. The Confederates opened fire, and after token resistance Sumter surrendered. The catalytic agent had been provided. Virginia, Arkansas, Tennessee, and North Carolina promptly left the Union. Lincoln called for 75,000 volunteers to put down the "insurrection" and a tidal wave of patriotic emotion swept North and South alike. The most savage conflict of the century began in a holiday mood.

Both sides expected that one battle would bring quick and easy victory. The North had better reasons for optimism. It had more than a two-to-one edge in manpower and almost all of the nation's industrial plants. There were no railroad repair shops in the South, no mills that produced woolen cloth, no shoe or glass factories, and no facilities for producing needles, pins, matches, or even salt. The Confederacy, however, was the world's leading producer of cotton and counted on English and French intervention to prevent the shutdown of European mills. The Confederates also were fighting for the most part on their own territory.

General Winfield Scott, the aged hero of the Mexican War, who still was commander of the U.S. Army, was one of the few who predicted that the war would be long and bloody and could be won only by a gradual constriction of Southern territory, combined with a naval blockade of Confederate ports. Scott's "anaconda" plan was greeted with hilarity and jeers on all sides.

That, of course, was the way it finally worked out, but during the first two years the South stunned the Union with a series of brilliant victories on the scrubby terrain lying between the rival capitals of Washington and Richmond. The first major engagement, at Bull Run, ended with the rout of General Irvin McDowell's green troops and a mad flight back to Washington of the Congressmen and ladies who had come to watch the fun. George McClellan, jaunty and arrogant, succeeded Scott. Despite Lincoln's impatience ("McClellan has the slows"), Little Mac built the Army of the Potomac into a professional fighting force and, after endless postponements, finally set out to capture Richmond. He met Robert E. Lee instead. In a week of pitched battles Lee harried, outguessed, and outmaneuvered his cautious opponent, and only clumsy staff work by the Confederates prevented them from bagging the Union army.

Lincoln next named Henry Halleck to the top command and John Pope head of the newly created Army of Virginia. Pope grandiloquently announced that his headquarters were in his saddle—a statement that caused observers to remark that his headquarters were where his hindquarters should have been—and soon thereafter was overwhelmed by Lee and Thomas J. "Stonewall" Jackson at the Second Battle of Bull Run. Lee then set out to invade the North, and McClellan was hastily recalled. Astonishingly, a set of Lee's orders was lost and stumbled upon by Union soldiers. Waving the orders jubilantly, McClellan said, "Here is a paper with which, if I cannot whip Bobby Lee, I will be willing to go home."

Even with this edge, McClellan, by caution and hesitation, blew a once-in-a-lifetime opportunity to destroy the Confederate Army piecemeal. Lee discovered what had happened, called his scattered forces together and fought the Union to a near draw in a dreadful day of slaughter on a ridge overlooking Antietam Creek in Maryland.

The Battle of Antietam was close enough to a Northern victory, however, to induce Lincoln to play a political trump card, the Emancipation Proclamation. By freeing Southern slaves, it gave Northerners, many of whom were beginning to wonder what they were fighting for, an issue and a cause. Issuance of the Proclamation killed Southern hopes of foreign intervention once and for all. Factory workers overseas, making it clear they would not handle cotton picked by slave labor, rallied to the Northern cause and obliged would-be interventionists to think twice about aiding the South.

In the West, Union victories were the rule rather than the exception. Early in 1862, Ulysses S. Grant electrified the country when he demanded and accepted the unconditional surrender of two key forts controlling access to a long stretch of the Mississippi River. Within the next year, Nashville and Memphis were lost to the Confederacy. Missouri and Kentucky were brought safely into the Union, while Texas and Arkansas became increasingly isolated from their sister states east of the great river. By the spring of 1863 Grant, a head-down fighter, called off his attempts to storm Vicksburg, the last Southern bastion on the river, and besieged the town and the 30,000 Confederate troops trapped within its perimeters. On July 4, Vicksburg surrendered and the Mississippi, as Lincoln put it, ran "unvexed to the sea."

On that same day the last hope of a Southern victory ended on Pennsylvania farmlands. In June, Lee had invaded the North for the second time in an effort to divert Northern regiments from Vicksburg. He met the Union army, now commanded by George Meade, near the town of Gettysburg. Three days of brutal and often hand-to-hand fighting followed. More than 43,000 men (over one fourth the total engaged) became casualties. On July 3, Lee sent 15,000 veteran troops across vast open fields in a final desperate assault on the Union lines. It was a gallant but hopeless move, and when the survivors staggered back to the Confederate positions, the climax of the war had been reached.

The conflict dragged on for nearly two more years, increasingly destructive and increasingly professional.

With Grant in overall charge of the Union armies and a new breed of general—William Sherman, Philip Sheridan, and George Thomas, among them—taking orders from him, the North settled down to the grim job of winning the war by attrition. The strategy was simple: to hold Lee's army on the defensive while the anaconda did its work elsewhere.

In 1864, in a series of murderously costly pitched battles in the Virginia wilderness, the Army of the Potomac pushed Lee's tattered troops step by step back toward Richmond, a campaign that ended in a siege when an attempt to break through Southern lines at Petersburg failed. For months the opposing forces faced one another in entrenchments that were sometimes as close as thirty yards. Simultaneously, Phil Sheridan's troopers ravaged the Shenandoah Valley, Lee's breadbasket, from one end to the other.

In Tennessee, the battles of Lookout Mountain and Missionary Ridge opened Georgia to invasion. The coils tightened inexorably on Atlanta and before long Sherman's "bummers" took over the blazing shell of the Confederacy's largest rail center. Without pause, they marched southeast, burning, looting, and tearing up rail lines (winding them around tree trunks into "Sherman neckties") as they went. Savannah fell—a New Year's present for newly re-elected Lincoln—and Sherman's army marched north into South Carolina, leaving a swath of desolation behind it.

The end, mercifully, came in the spring of 1865. With his last railroad supply line about to be cut, Lee abandoned Richmond and attempted to escape westward. Grant caught up to him, however, and at Appomattox Courthouse on Palm Sunday the surrender came. The remnants of other Southern armies—armies was no longer the name for them—laid down their rifles a few days later.

It was a terrible and tragic war, and the supreme tragedy, which took place just five days after Lee's surrender, was the assassination of the President. However wily and pragmatic the prewar Lincoln may have been, he grew mightily in stature, both as a human being and a statesman, during his years in office. First and last, he was a Unionist who deeply believed that the bonds which held the individual states together were indissoluble, and that the erring sisters should be brought back into the fold with understanding and compassion. It is idle to speculate whether he would have succeeded or failed; certainly lust for revenge was widespread in the North. But it is permissible to conclude that Southern recovery would have been far more rapid and that much of the heartache of the past hundred years would have been avoided if Lincoln had lived.

As it turned out, the new President, Andrew Johnson, while well-intentioned, was no match for the hate-mongers, and a period of repression—Reconstruction, we call it ironically—was visited on the luckless South. The days of carpetbaggers brought with them widespread corruption, and the attempt to put blacks who had never learned to write or read into public office created an inevitable backlash. The rise of the Ku Klux Klan and other secret gangs of night riders reestablished white supremacy within ten years of Appomattox, terrified the black population, and created a pattern of distrust between the races that persists to this day.

What did the Civil War accomplish? First, it vastly increased the power of the Federal Government. Second, it established that the rights of states did not include the privilege of secession. Third, it made possible the eventual industrialization of the South—although it is likely that slavery would have died of its inherent weaknesses and that urbanization would have come even if there had been no fighting. Finally, blacks won their freedom but precious little else. Black ghettos, busing, the rising tide of crime, Martin Luther King, Medgar Evers, and more are part of the Civil War heritage.

Of the 2,200,000 Northerners who joined the fight, more than 650,000 became casualties. Deaths totalled around 365,000, the wounded only 283,000—an astonishing fact, for in later wars the proportions were just the other way around. The reasons, of course, lay in the primitive state of surgery and antisepsis. An abdominal wound caused by a Minié ball that tore into a man's guts was an almost certain death sentence, and even bullets lodged in a man's arm or leg too often meant amputation, with death from infection a likely result.

As for the South, no figures are available, but it is probable that at least 800,000 men saw service and that the proportion of dead and wounded was higher than for Northern troops. In other words, nearly a million men—one out of every thirteen white males in the country in 1860—became casualties of the war.

There were other effects as well. For the first time in U.S. military history black troops served in the army. For the first time American troops systematically undertook a scorched-earth policy, engaged generally in trench warfare, and used observation balloons in battle.

Finally, and perhaps most important of all, the war gave voice to one of the most eloquent sentences ever written:

"With malice toward none; with charity for all; with firmness in the right, as God gives us to see the right, let us strive on to finish the work we are in; to bind up the nation's wounds; to care for him who shall have borne the battle, and for his widow and his orphan— to do all which may achieve and cherish a just, and a lasting peace, among ourselves and with all nations."

—Abraham Lincoln,
Second Inaugural Address

Union major-general and his staff.

Young Georgian, Private Thomas
Jefferson Ruskin (opposite), met his death
in brambled thickets of Chancellorsville
in May, 1863. Above: Men of the 8th
New York State Militia.

Below: Bandmaster of 3rd New Hampshire
Infantry in comfortable surroundings
at Hilton Head, S.C., headquarters.
Opposite: Golden-haired Capt. George A.
Custer, whose last stand was fourteen years
in the future, with Confederate prisoner
and black boy in 1862 (top, l).
Drummer boy near Harper's Ferry, Va. (top,
r). Cooks' galley of Company K,
3rd New Hampshire Infantry (bottom).

JAMES GIBSON/LIBRARY OF CONGRESS

LIBRARY OF CONGRESS

H. P. MOORE/NEW HAMPSHIRE HISTORICAL SOCIETY

31

Opposite: Field artillery, mortars, and
cannonballs lined up along beach of
Yorktown, Va. Confederates abandoned town
in May, 1862, and it became staging
area for Gen. McClellan's ill-fated effort
to capture Richmond.
Above: Guns grew bigger as war
dragged on. Following pages: Federal
Horse Artillery, Peninsular Campaign, 1862.

TIMOTHY H. O'SULLIVAN

Preceding pages: Northern dead after
first day's fighting at Gettysburg, 1863.
Below: Dead Confederate in trenches
at Petersburg, Va., just before war's end.
Right: Dead Confederate after
hand-to-hand fighting at Spotsylvania
Court House, Va., in spring 1864, one
of the most savage battles of the war.

LIBRARY OF CONGRESS

TIMOTHY H. O'SULLIVAN

Charleston, S.C., after visit by
Sherman's "bummers" in spring, 1865.
Sherman's army cut a wide swath of ruin
and desolation as it marched north
from Savannah in war's final months.
Charleston was particularly hard
hit because Union troops held South
Carolinians responsible for starting war.

FRANCO-PRUSSI

N WAR 1870-1871

In the year 1860, what came to be known as the Second Reich was regarded by the rest of the world as comic-opera country—a crazy jumble of duchies and grand duchies, free cities, petty kingdoms, and principalities, each independent and jealous of the other. In the minds of outlanders, it was the place where Santa Claus had originated, a land of jovial, beer-swilling burgomasters in *lederhosen* and plump, beribboned *maedschen*.

Never was a picture more misleading. The political patchwork between the Rhine and the Oder resulted from humiliating defeats early in the century at the hands of Napoleon's armies, which had left many Germans with feelings of frustration and military inferiority.

Wilhelm I, who ascended the throne of Prussia in 1861, reunited the scattered states and reminded Germans that their military heritage dated back nearly two millennia, to the days when Germanic tribesmen brought the advance of Roman legions to an abrupt halt in the dark and forbidding forests of their homeland. In pursuing his goal of reunification, the bleakly conservative Wilhelm surrounded himself with a trio of equally reactionary but brilliant lieutenants: Otto von Bismarck, the political planner; Helmuth von Moltke, the military genius; and Alfred Krupp, an eccentric armorer.

In short order, Wilhelm imposed upon Prussia a large, conscript army whose jackboots and spiked helmets became symbols of a war machine that terrified the world for eight decades. In 1864 the Soldier King sent his new army on its path to glory. Allied with Austria, Prussia attacked and wrung from tiny Denmark the duchies of Schleswig and Holstein. The Prussian army was expanded and two years later was at war with Austria, plus Bavaria, Hanover, Saxony, Baden, and Württemberg. It was no contest at all. Inside of seven weeks, Moltke had transported huge forces by railroad boxcar (a trick he picked up from Union generals in the Civil War) to the Bohemian fortress of Königgrätz, where they overwhelmed the luckless Austrians and their allies. Wilhelm promptly annexed Silesia and nearly all of North Germany.

The rest of Europe found all of this mildly amusing. Who would have thought the pumpernickels, as the Prussians were affectionately called, could do it? But then, of course, Denmark was nothing. As for the Austrians, well, everyone beat the Austrians and had been doing so for centuries. Napoleon III, Emperor of France, found Prussian antics annoying rather than funny. A few years later, when Bismarck tried to install a Hohenzollern prince on the Spanish throne to succeed the recently expelled nymphomaniac Queen Isabella II, Napoleon indulged in noisy saber rattling. Wilhelm implied that he might retract, but Louis Napoleon, with an instinctive talent for self-destruction, ignored the overture and demanded a royal apology from Germany.

He didn't get it. Bismarck edited the telegraphic refusal to apologize that Wilhelm had dictated from Ems spa into a slap on both of Napoleon's cheeks. Worse yet, he sent copies to other rulers around Europe. Under nineteenth-century diplomatic rules, Napoleon had no choice but war, which was precisely what Bismarck and Moltke wanted.

To observers of the European scene, Louis Napoleon and his empire presented an impressive façade. Like his uncle, the great Bonaparte, Louis was jaunty, arrogant, and an acknowledged military expert. Unlike Bonaparte, he was extremely stupid. As for his army, it appeared to be better than it was. His troops had routed the Austrians only ten years before at Magenta and Solferino, and had acquitted themselves well on dozens of other battlefields in the Crimea, Africa, and Mexico. French troops and French military techniques were held to be far and away the best in the world. They weren't.

On Bastille Day, 1870, on the afternoon of the day he received the Ems dispatch, Napoleon ordered mobilization. So did Wilhelm.

No outside military observer gave Wilhelm's forces a chance. All expected an immediate invasion of Prussia—as did a number of Prussian cities which began to collect French tricolors with which to greet the invaders. Generals Sheridan and Burnside came all the way from the United States to witness the rout, and the London *Times* told its readers to bet every shilling they had on "Casquette against Pumpernickel." As for the French army itself, reared on memories of Austerlitz and Marengo, its élan was magnificent. For them it was to be the kind of war one saw in Meissonier's paintings—flashing sabers, bayonet charges, cavalry leaping over the hedges in pursuit of fleeing Germans.

The upset developed with nightmarish speed.

Preceding pages: Panoramic view
of elaborate French fortifications in Alsace
after seizure by Germans.

The first big battle took place at Worth in northeastern France. Within hours it became apparent how tragically the French had erred in placing their faith in small arms, infantry charges, and hand-to-hand conflict. French ordnance experts had turned down Krupp's salesmen and stuck with brass-barreled guns which had less than half the range of Krupp's breechloading steel cannon. French infantry, exposed and helpless, milled about in confusion under a pitiless rain of steel, waiting for the charge that never came. By nightfall, the French were in full retreat and the *Marseillaise* had changed to a new chant: *"Un, deux, trois, merde."*

The rest was more of the same. One French army was penned up in Metz, but the major disaster came at Sedan, where the German High Command watched from a hillside as its long-range guns pulverized the forces of the French Emperor. Within three days, McMahon's army surrendered and Louis Napoleon was bundled off to a German *stalag*. France declared herself a Republic and organized a last-ditch defense of Paris, digging in behind a thirty-foot wall, a moat, and 3,000 antiquated brass cannon. Within ten days, French railroads carried Moltke's armies to Château-Thierry and Paris's last link with the outside world was cut. For a hundred and fourteen days thereafter, German guns poured shells into the helpless city. Tens of thousands were left homeless, and the number of killed and maimed by shelling was enormous. In January, Paris surrendered.

The war dead were approximately 90,000, of whom more than 50,000 were French. While the cost in lives was small, compared to later wars, the results were portentous. The emergence of the Second Reich as the preeminent military power on the continent of Europe inevitably led to new alliances and new big-power combinations. The easy victory left Germany's rulers convinced of its military superiority *über alles*, a frame of mind that took two wars and the combined strength of the greater part of the rest of the world to dispel. The loss of Alsace-Lorraine left the French with a burning desire for revenge—an emotion that Clemenceau exploited fully at Versailles forty-seven years later.

Finally, the war marked the coming of age of the Industrial Revolution in warfare. Germany's railroads, planned with the movement of troops in mind, and Germany's steel guns were the precursors of the airplanes, trucks, tanks, and Big Berthas of World War I, and the atomic bomb in the greater holocaust that followed.

Above: Prussian troops parading through French town. Right: Members of French unit personally equipped and commanded by le Duc de Chartres—an echo of an earlier military age. Opposite, top: Victorious German infantry after killing or capturing 20,000 French soldiers in Battle of Champigny. Bottom: French encampment at Metz.

Extraordinary photograph of combat
—German troops are firing toward camera—
during crucial Battle of Sedan. Right:
German soldiers clowning in
captured French fort. Opposite: Though
outgunned by enemy's artillery,
French did have a few heavy "fortress"
cannon like this one in action,
probably outside of Paris.

From l to r: French medical
corpsman; German medic; member
of the *Milice*, or French
home guard, during siege of Paris;
postwar French propaganda postcard shows
provinces of Alsace and Lorraine
weeping for their lost homeland. Below:
Hotel de Ville, city hall of Paris,
destroyed by shelling during siege.

BRITISH COLONIA

WARS 1882-1902

The more or less tranquil century between Waterloo and the assassination of the Archduke Ferdinand at Sarajevo saw the British empire grow to a size unparalleled in history. The era has been called the *Pax Britannica*, a latter-day version of the *Pax Romana*, during which Rome's emperors ruled territories from Spain to India. The analogy has its virtues. Great Britain was the manufacturing headquarters for most of the world, and her navy two or three times the size of its nearest rivals. In many parts of the globe the mere presence of a few Britishers was enough to keep the peace.

Those decades have come down to us pleasantly romanticized by motion pictures and books: cavalry charges with naked swords glittering in the desert sun; jungles full of chattering monkeys and painted savages; shaded stretches of green lawn in remote corners of the world where tropical stillness was broken only by the pounding hooves of polo ponies, the crack of a ball on a cricket bat, and the murmur of well-modulated British voices. The only trouble with this pleasant composite of the age, in which people talked about the White Man's Burden without laughing, is that it did not quite conform to fact, for *Pax Britannica* wasn't really as placid as it sounds.

Throughout the nineteenth century, world maps grew progressively dotted with pink, like a child coming down with measles. Pink was the color used to show the possessions of Her Majesty, Victoria Regina, during whose long rule most of England's ministers pursued a "Forward Policy" that added vast stretches of land and millions of new subjects—black, brown, and yellow—to her empire. In these pages we have room, however, for only two of the British adventures that broke the *Pax Britannica*.

KHARTOUM TO OMDURMAN 1882–1896

Thirteen years after the Suez Canal was opened in 1869, the British government, alarmed at the activities of a new strong man in Egypt, sent a fleet to bombard Alexandria. Shortly thereafter all of Egypt was taken in hand.

Britain soon discovered that she had a large crocodile by the tail. Centuries of misrule had left the country a pesthouse, her citizenry illiterate, impoverished, and over-taxed, her army a joke, her public officials crooks and cutthroats. Most difficult of all was the problem of the Sudan, a vast, arid land to the south, over which Egyptian whips had cracked for centuries. The sprawling town of Khartoum, near the confluence of the Blue and White Niles, was the funnel through which merchandise flowed northward. The merchandise ranged from ostrich plumes and ivory to the area's most profitable commodity, human beings, and Khartoum had long been headquarters for the slave trade.

Although the Egyptian government publicly disapproved of slavery, it measured the success of its representatives in Khartoum by the amount of money they could extort from slavers, and the rapaciousness of the Egyptian overseers exceeded belief.

A savior arose to free the Sudanese from their Egyptian oppressors. His name was Mohammed Ahmed, and his followers believed he was the Mahdi, the long-awaited Redeemer of Islam. The Mahdist revolt began in 1881 and spread like prairie fire through the land. The Egyptian army under British command sent to stamp out the movement was annihilated by the Mahdi, and in 1883 the British decided it was time to get out of the Sudan. To insure the safe removal of Egyptian garrisons and to make the best peace possible, Charles George Gordon, a former governor of the Sudan, was sent to Khartoum. Gordon was one of the remarkable men Victorian England produced in such abundance to conduct the affairs of empire and fight her wars. From the Crimea to China (where he led the legendary "Ever-Victorious Army" in suppressing the Taiping Rebellion) to Khartoum, "Chinese" Gordon cut a wide swath.

Now his thoroughness in supervising the evacuation proved his undoing. The Mahdi's army of dervishes surrounded Khartoum, trapping Gordon behind its defenses. Some measure of his qualities of leadership can be judged from the fact that his army of 7,000 and the 30,000 inhabitants of Khartoum, nearly all of whom were Mohammedan and would normally have joined the Mahdi cause, remained loyal to him for nearly a year while the town held off its attackers.

After a long period of vacillation, the British government bestirred itself and sent a relief column to Gordon's rescue. As the rescue party approached the town the Mahdists broke into Khartoum. In the massacre that followed, Gordon was cut to pieces and his head carried in triumph to the Mahdi.

Preceding pages:
Boers sight Long Tom artillery
piece at siege of Mafeking.

The British relief force retreated to Egypt and the entire Sudan was left to the rule of the insurgents.

For more than ten years thereafter, with Gordon's hideous death a matter of painful recollection, the British stubbornly proceeded to institute a host of changes to improve irrigation, combat disease, and weed out corruption. They also built up an Egyptian army that was not only well-trained but would actually fight.

In 1892, Horatio Herbert Kitchener was named sirdar, or commander in chief, of the new army. He was another remarkable Britisher, daring, energetic, and capable. Four years later he set out to retake the Sudan. His campaign was a succession of victories. After each one, railway tracks were laid behind the advance to bring up supplies. By September, 1898, the final goal was reached—the new city of Omdurman, site of the sacred tomb of the Mahdi, who had died in 1885.

The Battle of Omdurman was a rout, quickly followed by the capture of Khartoum. Kitchener lost 482 officers and men, and the Mahdists more than 30,000 dead, wounded, or captured. After Omdurman the Mahdist leader met his death when the remnants of his army were rounded up far to the south. Once more a huge, new patch of pink was added to the world map—the Anglo-Egyptian Sudan.

THE BOER WAR 1899–1902

The industrious Dutch settlers of South Africa first arrived in the seventeenth century. Excellent farmers—"Boers"—and rigid Calvinists, they combined caution with outbursts of wild daring, energy with stubbornness, conservatism with a distaste for African blacks. In 1834, when the British in the Cape Colony freed their slaves, the Boers emigrated rather than conform.

The Great Trek, as it was called, resulted in the establishment of two Boer republics, the Transvaal and the Orange Free State. By virtue of a special treaty with the British, they were nominally independent, but after gold was discovered in the Transvaal, a flood of British prospectors poured in. By 1895 the *Uitlanders*, meaning foreigners, equaled the native Boers in number and paid almost all of the taxes. Nonetheless, the Boers refused to grant them political rights.

Fighting began in 1899, after negotiations between the British high commissioner and Paul Kruger, president of the Transvaal, broke down with Kruger in tears saying, "It is our country you want!" Thirty-five thousand Boers invaded British territory. They had no uniforms, but they had everything else. Almost all were mounted and crack shots. They had better artillery than the British and in the beginning outnumbered them. In short order, 10,000 British troops were cooped up in Ladysmith, another smaller force was surrounded and besieged in Mafeking. Three crack British divisions were landed and crushed in turn. When "Black Week," as the British press termed it, was mentioned to Queen Victoria, that ancient lady said, "We are not interested in the possibilities of defeat. They do not exist."

More British troops were sent, more than 400,000 in all. Two great names in British colonial history arrived on the scene: Lord Roberts of Kandahar, hero of the Afghan wars, and Lord Kitchener of Khartoum. In England the country was swept up in a wave of patriotic feeling and "Marching on Pretoria" became virtually a national anthem. The tide turned quickly. Ladysmith and Kimberley were relieved early in 1900, and by midyear the siege of Mafeking was lifted and the Boer strongholds were in British hands.

The Boers refused to quit. Operating out of widely scattered farmhouses and hideouts deep in the veldt, they harried the British unmercifully with guerrilla attacks. Kitchener was placed in charge and resorted to concentration camps and a scorched-earth policy. More than 20,000 Boers died of disease in the hideously unsanitary camps, and Parliament rang with opposition charges of barbarism.

Finally, the Boers sued for peace. The terms were perhaps the most generous in the history of warfare and unquestionably accounted for the dedication of Boers to the British cause in the great world wars that followed. No one was punished. Self-government was promised the Boers, and Britain paid £3,000,000 in compensation.

Queen Victoria died more than a year before the final peace came. It is certain that she never had any doubt as to the outcome. What she did not realize was that the Transvaal and the Orange Free State marked the high tide of empire. The century that had just begun was to see the pink patches in world atlases disappear, one by one.

BOER WAR
British troops moving up-country
by railroad (top). Five-inch howitzer
at moment of firing (above). Boer
farm in flames (left). British
skirmish line at Brandwater Basin.

Boers (opposite and at siege of Ladysmith
below) were well-armed, determined,
and surprisingly successful
in early stages of war. It took full might of
empire—and Kitchener's leadership—
to bring about surrender (bottom).

RADIO TIMES HULTON PICTURE LIBRARY ▲

WAR IN THE SUDAN
Top: British officers observing Mahdist
forces before Battle of Omdurman. Opposite,
bottom right: Looting bodies of slain
after Omdurman victory. Bottom left: Capture
of Mahdi's successor, Mahmoud (in
bloodstained garment) at Atbara. Top:
Australian troops. Right: Camel caravan
hauling water to troops.

63

N WAR 1898-1899

The "splendid little war," as Secretary of State John Hay referred to the Spanish adventure, was the United States' first appearance as a world power. When it ended, the republic was also an empire.

For a number of years the burgeoning United States had been feeling its oats. An argument with Canada in 1887 over fishing rights caused a nameless bard, writing for the Detroit *News*, to rewrite a British music-hall jingle:

We do not want to fight
But by jingo, if we do,
We'll scoop in all the fishing grounds
And the whole Dominion, too.

The quarrel was patched up. So too were close brushes with Chile in 1891 and Great Britain in 1895 over Queen Victoria's continuing presence in British Guiana. When war failed to develop, young Theodore Roosevelt, then head of the New York City police board, wrote plaintively to his friend, the Massachusetts Senator Henry Cabot Lodge: "The clamor of the peace faction has convinced me that this country needs a war."

In 1895 a series of insurrections against Spanish rule broke out in Cuba which, along with Puerto Rico, was Spain's last outpost in the New World. An overwhelming percentage of Americans sided, as Americans have usually done, with the underdog. Cuba was the underdog to end under-dogs. For decades the population, part Spanish and part black, had been put upon by clumsy and venal overlords appointed by third-rate rulers in Madrid.

Soon after the American Civil War ended, stories of Spanish atrocities in Cuba began to appear in Ameri-can books and newspapers. They bore such captions as "The Massacre of the Young Students" or "Latest Blood-Chilling Spanish Horrors." Thus, when Madrid sent General Valeriano Weyler to suppress the latest revolt, most Americans expected the worst. They got it when Weyler herded masses of Cubans into terribly mismanaged concentration camps and earned for himself the title of "Butcher."

Weyler's behavior was a great boon to jour-nalists in the United States, two of whom, Pulitzer and Hearst, were fighting a knock-down-drag-out battle for circulation. Each day for weeks and months, headlines got bigger and stories of Spanish misdeeds became more lurid as the two titans of journalism strove to outdo one another. Joseph Pulitzer remarked that he rather liked the idea of a war. He didn't want a big one, just one big enough to allow him to "gauge the reflex in circulation figures." And William Randolph Hearst, once the conflict came, ran the proud headline in his New York paper: "How do you like The Journal's war?"

As the journalistic roars of protest grew louder, Spain hastily recalled Weyler and promised reforms. Then, just as the journalists were beginning to look for fresh headlines, the battleship *Maine*, which had been ordered to pay a "friendly" visit to Cuba, blew up in Havana harbor, with a loss of 260 men. The cause was never made known. The first American board of inquiry said the explosion had been external, but another board, thirteen years later, was divided. The majority claimed that the explosion had been external but not where the first board said it was, and the minority said it had been internal, as the Spaniards had always claimed. The *Maine* was eventually towed into deep water and sunk. All requests by Spain or by other nations to examine the evidence were refused.

All this was academic, however, for Congress and the American public were fighting mad, and under their pressure President McKinley's earlier resolve to avoid war rapidly faded. His message to Congress left the ultimate decision to the legislators, but barely mentioned that two days earlier Spain had offered to concede virtually everything the Americans might ask.

The United States' declaration of hostilities stated an intention to leave Cuba an independent nation when the war ended. It made no mention of other Spanish possessions, such as Puerto Rico and the Philippines, which Senator Lodge and others hoped to acquire. The nobility of the intentions toward Cuba, however, as opposed to what imperialist powers like Great Britain or Portugal would do, was sufficient to suffuse the entire nation in a warm glow of self-righteousness. The glow never faded, and the same ingenuousness that led Ameri-cans to believe that Cubans would be able to govern themselves in approved democratic fashion caused the public to anticipate a series of glorious and bloodless victories.

Of this naïve assumption Spain did not dis-

Preceding pages: 69th Regiment breaking
camp before embarking for Cuba.

abuse them. Less than a week after war was declared, Commodore George Dewey at Manila Bay gave an order straight out of the melodramas so popular at the time, "You may fire when ready, Gridley." No one quite knew who or what Gridley was (he was the commanding officer of the Asiatic Fleet flagship), but the fact that the U. S. Navy had sunk virtually the entire Spanish Oriental command—ten men-of-war—without the loss of a single American or ship was only what was expected.

This one-sided result was exactly what Senator Lodge feared when writing to Lieutenant-Colonel Theodore Roosevelt, of the Rough Riders: "For various reasons I am not anxious to see the war jammed through . . . let us get the outlying things first." The outlying things, among others, were Puerto Rico and Hawaii.

Within a few weeks the balance of the Spanish navy under Admiral Cervera was bottled up in Santiago harbor. The only way to get it out was to land American troops on Cuban shores. The War Department, through a series of incredible snafus, tried hard to obey Lodge's warning not to jam things through. The 16,000 troops eventually put ashore in Cuba had been obliged to commandeer their own freight cars to reach the port of embarkation. Once aboard, they had been left on deck for days in broiling sun and, after landing, were fed spoiled tinned meat. Although fewer than 400 died of wounds in the entire war, the number stricken with ptomaine poisoning or yellow fever ran into the thousands.

Roosevelt's Rough Riders (whose horses, through another High Command goof, had been left behind in Florida) stole the show. They made a magnificent charge on foot up San Juan Hill and into the mouth of Spanish cannon. Although the skirmish was inconclusive, Cervera decided to attempt an escape before Santiago fell. Two days after the Rough Riders' charge, Spain's wooden fleet made its dash for safety. It never had a chance. As the ships reached open water one after another was blown to splinters by American guns. Cervera and hundreds of his men were plucked from the burning wreckage. Within another few weeks Spanish troops in Cuba and Puerto Rico threw down their arms and the unequal war was over.

When the peace treaty was finally signed in April, 1899, one year after hostilities had started, the United States found itself in possession of Puerto Rico, Hawaii, Guam, and the entire Philippine archipelago. It took more than three years and more money and human lives than had the war with Spain to crush an insurrection of Philippine guerrillas, but, most Americans told themselves philosophically, this was part of the White Man's Burden.

As for brave little Cuba, the United States made good its promise to withdraw, but not without a few strings attached that irritated Cuban patriots up to the time of Fidel Castro. An amendment to the Cuban constitution gave the United States the right to intervene at any time to maintain an "adequate government for the protection of life, liberty and property" and to keep a naval base at Guantanamo and coaling stations along the coast. Apart from these concessions, the Cubans were permitted to work out their own future—a future that led eventually to the Bay of Pigs.

Above: Officers of U.S.S. *Maine*, whose
mysterious sinking in Havana harbor brought
on the war. Opposite: U.S.S. *New York*, 8200-ton
armored cruiser, was Rear-Admiral William T.
Sampson's flagship during blockade of
Cuba, but missed Battle of Santiago Bay.

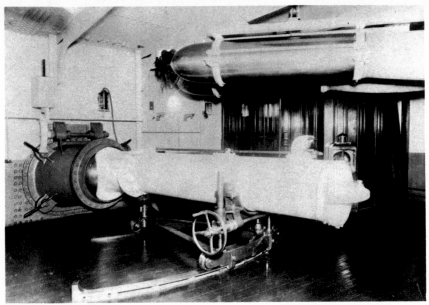

Below: Stricken *Maine*. Curiously, no inquiry ever determined the cause of the fatal blast. *Maine* was towed to deep water and sunk. Left: One of *Maine's* torpedo tubes. Opposite: Hulk of the *Mercedes*, one of aged Spanish ships shot out of the water as fleet attempted to escape from Santiago Bay.

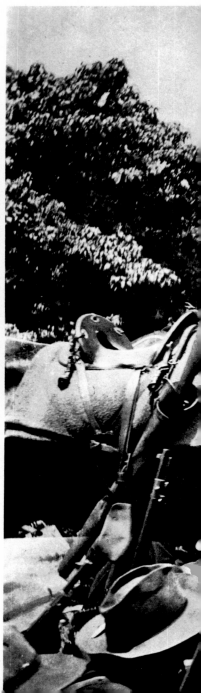

Above: American ammunition cart in
Philippines. Opposite: Two scenes of
successful American assault on San Juan
Hill in Cuba. Top: Dug in. Bottom:
16th Infantry under fire.

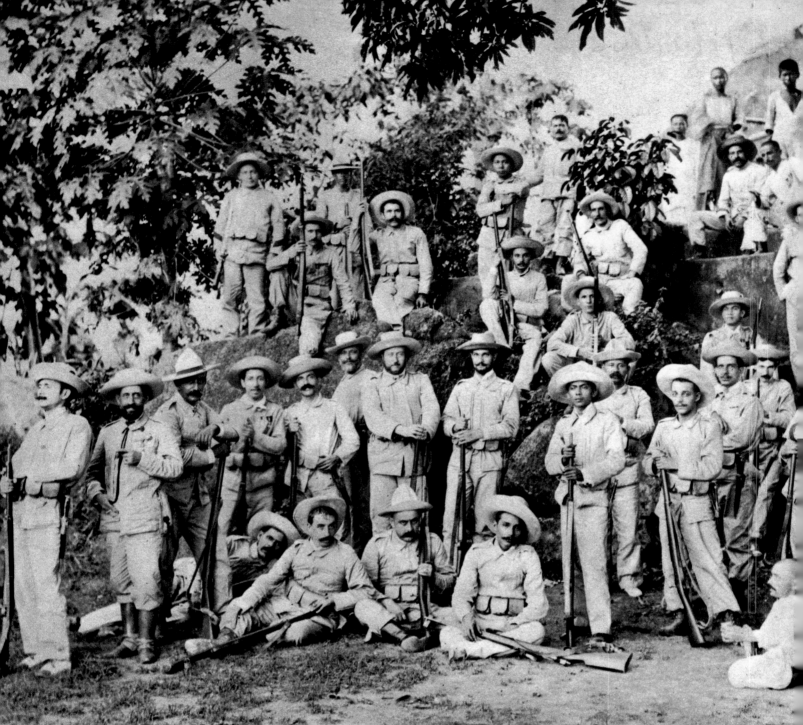

Above: Volunteers serving Spain in
Philippines. Opposite: Stereopticon view
—probably posed—of 4th Infantry
(top) presumably repulsing Spanish attack
in Philippines. Bottom: American gun
position overlooking Manila.

JAMES M. DAVIS,
New York, St. Louis, Liverpool, Toronto, Sydney.

Copyright 1900, by B. W. Kilburn.

PHILIPPINE

13481. Aim! Ready! Fire! The 4th Infantry Boys repulsing an attack at Imus Luzon, P. I.

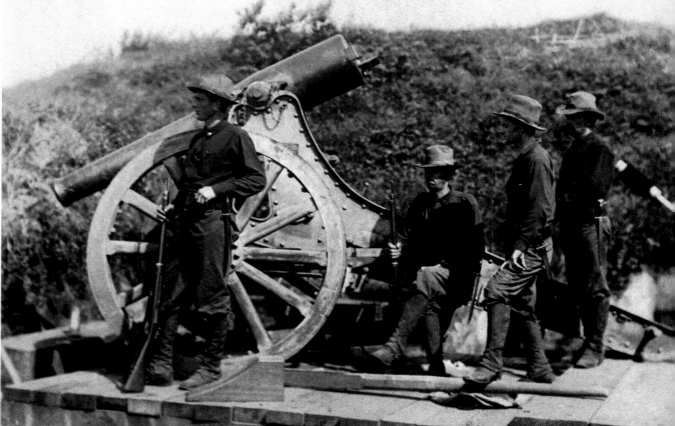

RUSSO-JAPANES

E WAR 1904-1905

When word reached Tsar Nicholas II that his Baltic fleet had been wiped out by the Japanese in the Strait of Tsushima, he stuffed the dispatch in his pocket and went on playing tennis. There was something highly significant in the gesture, not only as an indication of the shallowness of Nicholas's mind, but also because it represented, in a sense, the apathy and annoyance of the Russian people for an unwanted and unwelcome war.

As Russia entered the twentieth century, the country seethed on the brink of revolution. A period of far-reaching liberal reform had ended abruptly in 1881 with the assassination of Tsar Alexander II. The years that followed were characterized by reaction and repression, famines and pogroms, and terrorist activities. Vladimir Ilyich Ulyanov, later known as Lenin, was writing tracts that were eventually to become the Holy Writ of Marxism, while other liberal and revolutionary groups were making elaborate but generally ineffectual plans for the overthrow of the monolithic Romanov dynasty.

To keep the lid on the bubbling unrest Nicholas appointed Vyacheslav Plehve, a harsh and obtuse police official, minister of Russia's internal affairs. Before he was killed by a terrorist bomb in 1904, Plehve urged the Tsar to start a "small, victorious war," pointing out that an appeal to the natural patriotism of the Russian people was a sure-fire way to stop political agitation. Nicholas liked the idea, particularly if the war could be fought in the Far East, where Russian interests were growing.

A few years earlier Japan had defeated China in a brief war, gained possession of the Liaotung Peninsula controlling the approaches to Tientsin and Peking, and then, to her dismay, was obliged to give it up in the face of Russian, German, and French pressure. In 1896 and 1898, Russia secured rights from China to continue the Trans-Siberian Railroad across Manchuria to terminals at Vladivostok and Mukden, a lease on the Liaotung Peninsula, and permission to construct a naval base at its tip, Port Arthur.

With Russian soldiers guarding the railway, Nicholas felt the time was right to move into Korea and acquire timber concessions. When he was warned that the move was almost certain to bring a Japanese reaction, Nicholas went ahead, with the enthusiastic backing of his cousin, the Kaiser.

Japan also had interests in Korea and, with a war party firmly in the saddle, prepared to land troops on the Asian mainland. The Russians attempted a bluff, ordering their antiquated naval squadron at Port Arthur to put to sea but then recalling it. The Japanese, who had no thought of bluffing, sent their fleet to sea and launched a surprise attack on the Russians—a performance that was to be repeated even more effectively against the Americans nearly four decades later at Pearl Harbor. Both countries formally declared war.

The first major engagement, late in April, 1904, was the Battle of the Yalu, in northern Korea. It set the pattern for all that was to follow and proved that Prussian-trained Japanese troops were more than a match for the Tsar's forces. The Russians were badly equipped with clumsy, ill-fitting boots, packs that weighed sixty pounds or more, and long coats that tripped them when they walked. Most of them were illiterate and hadn't the slightest idea what they were fighting for or against. They fought bravely, but ended up on the losing end of every battle.

The Japanese next laid siege to the Russian stronghold at Port Arthur. After eight months and enormous losses on both sides, the garrison surrendered, opening up the entire Liaotung Peninsula to Japan. The scene then shifted to Manchuria, where a series of battles stretched over two months and involved nearly a million men, ending with more than 100,000 Russian casualties and the fall of Mukden.

The last great battle of the war had more than a slight comic-opera touch to it. The Tsar ordered his Baltic fleet to sail for the Orient. While still in the North Sea, the edgy Russian sailors mistook a covey of British fishing smacks for Japanese warships and opened fire on them, an episode that nearly turned the conflict into an Anglo-Russo-Japanese war. Thereafter, the fleet continued its shameful voyage around the tip of Africa toward Vladivostok. Six months after its departure from home, it sailed into Japanese waters, where Admiral Heihachiro Togo's fleet was waiting for it in the Strait of Tsushima. There, in an afternoon and night, almost the entire Russian fleet was sunk or captured.

By now the Japanese had a problem, the same that Hitler was to experience in 1941. Although the Russian bear had been whipped every time, it stubbornly refused to stop fighting. There were still nearly a million Russian soldiers under arms and, worse yet, a seemingly endless flow of replacements streaming eastward on the Trans-Siberian Railroad.

At this juncture the Japanese secretly approached their good friend and booster, President Theodore Roosevelt. "I was thoroughly pleased with the Japanese victory," the former Rough Rider had written early in the war, "for Japan is playing our game." He arranged a meeting between Japanese and Russian leaders at Portsmouth, New Hampshire. The Russians did a much better job of bargaining than they had done as warriors. While the Treaty of Portsmouth gave Japan the Liaotung Peninsula and the southern part of Sakhalin Island, acknowledged Korea to be in Japan's sphere of interest, and led to the Russian evacuation of Manchuria, Russia managed to keep the Amur region and the areas in and around the Maritime Province, which had been its main foothold in the Far East for decades.

The war was a purely imperialistic struggle for Chinese and Korean territory, underwritten and made possible by French loans to Russia and Anglo-American credits to Japan.

Roosevelt and the Kaiser, who felt they had arranged the whole affair, were in truth puppets whose strings were being pulled by France and England—two countries that in a few years would unite against Germany.

The cost of the war was high in terms of human life. The Japanese admitted to more than 630,000 casualties; Russian losses were almost certainly close to a million.

On the home front the unpopular war badly undermined the prestige of Nicholas II. In January, 1905, an orderly crowd of striking workers from the Putilov metallurgical works marched on the Winter Palace in St. Petersburg to protest working conditions and pay. They were led by an Orthodox priest, Father Gapon. As the huge crowd pushed forward, police and troops guarding the palace panicked and fired into the crowd, killing 130, and wounding hundreds more. Even though the Tsar had not been in the palace and knew nothing of the demonstration, "Bloody Sunday" was attributed to his orders. "We have no Tsar any more," Father Gapon said. "Rivers of blood separate the Tsar from the people."

Opposite: Japanese troops moving into
position for siege of Port Arthur (top).
Bottom: Emergence of well-equipped,
Prussian-trained Japanese army as first-rate
military power startled the world.
Above: Russian reinforcements advancing
along route of Chinese imperial railway.

ssian naval officers—long
nort on performance. Opposite:
p disintegrating under Japanese
ent in famous Battle of Tsushima
iral Togo's fleet executed classic,
ssful maneuver known as "Crossing
ling its battle line to fire
t Russians, while Russian column
fire a few forward guns.

Opposite: Japanese batteries firing on
Russian position in siege of Port Arthur.
Below: Japanese infantry crouches in
shallow trench awaiting signal to charge.
Probably a staged rehearsal.

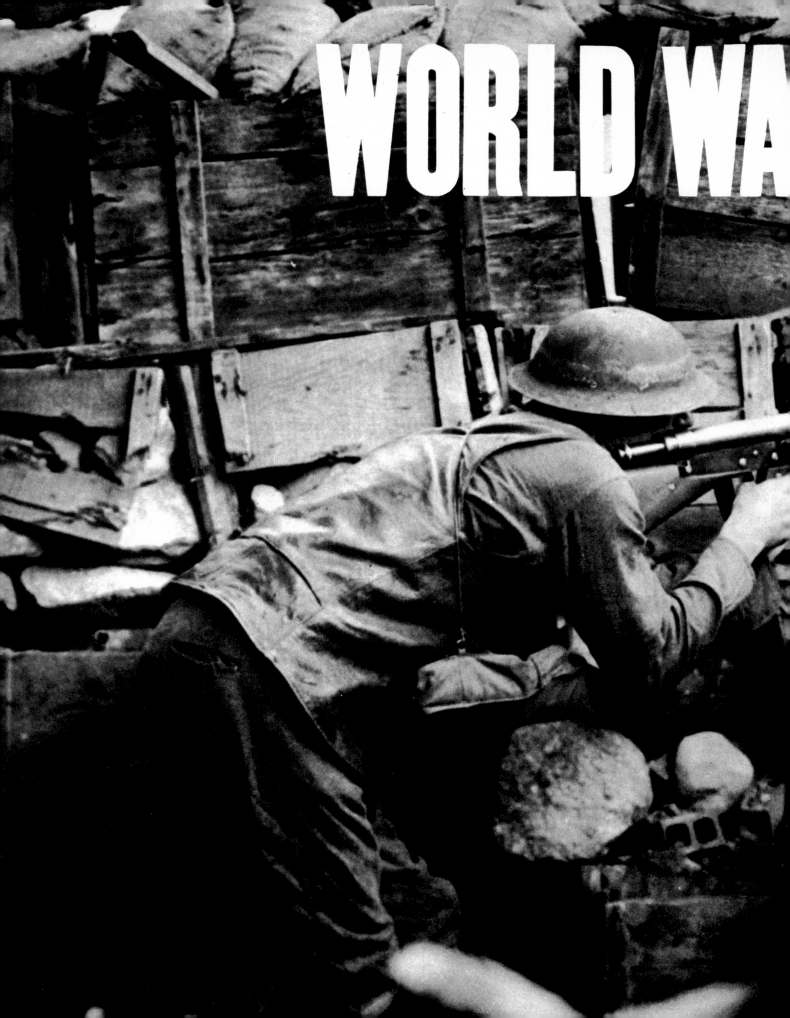

WORLD WA

R I 1914-1918

Of the millions who strolled in Europe's early summer sunshine of 1914, only those well into middle age could recall the time a major war had been fought on their continent. Nearly forty-four years had passed since German guns lobbed their last shell into a starving Paris, and it is only by assuming innocence in the young and forgetfulness in their elders that one can begin to understand the joy and exultation with which normally sane human beings sent their youngsters marching off to death—death that in most cases was as hideous as the nightmarish fantasies in a Bosch painting.

The First World War, a conflict immeasurably bigger than any the world had ever known, changed the face of the globe and continues to affect the lives of each of us today. It had its origins when Germany emerged from war with France in 1871 the strongest power on the Continent. For some years thereafter her diplomatic behavior was prudent and discreet. Under the stewardship of Chancellor Bismarck, the alliance with the Hapsburg dynasty of Austria-Hungary was expanded into the Triple Alliance, with Italy as the new partner, and friendly relations with Great Britain and Russia were encouraged. Then, with the ascension of Wilhelm II to the throne in 1888 and the subsequent removal of Bismarck, a new note began to echo through Europe's chancelleries. It was a note as strident and upsetting as the nasal indiscretions of Wilhelm himself.

Few rulers in world history have presented so many contradictions in terms as the new Kaiser. Beneath his endless assortment of military uniforms there beat the heart of a braggart and bully, just as his clinking spurs, gleaming sword and majestic cloak diverted attention from his shriveled left arm—a birth defect he tried to conceal. As for his mind, even the most impressive imperial trappings couldn't hide the fact that the All-Highest suffered from a bad case of verbosity and a habit of eternally ending up with his foot in his mouth. Toward England (he was the nephew of Edward VII), Wilhelm's attitude was particularly ambivalent, a queer mixture of love and hate, admiration and envy, suspicion and distrust.

The slogans of the day tell the story—"Blood and Iron," a "Place in the Sun," and *Gott mit uns.* The pace of munitions makers quickened, and German bellicosity soon brought about what she dreaded most—an alliance between France and Russia and the threat of war on two fronts. Soon after, as more and more capital ships of the new German high-seas fleet slid down the ways, an increasingly apprehensive England made a rapprochement with France which rapidly grew into a Triple Entente with Russia.

In the years before 1914, war in Europe had been narrowly avoided several times. After each brush with disaster the military strategists of each nation put their finishing touches on battle plans designed to bring quick victory once the fragile edifice of alliances and secret agreements came crashing down. The German plan, a product of the brilliant mind of Count Alfred von Schlieffen, called for a massive, scythe-like sweep of the army's right wing through Holland, Belgium, and northern France beyond Paris that would push the French forces eastward into the waiting guns of German armies in Alsace-Lorraine. It called for a six-week campaign after which the Germans would turn on Russia. Meanwhile, the Tsar's armies were to be held in check by skeleton forces on the eastern front. Schlieffen, like other German leaders, ignored the fact that Germany had solemnly guaranteed Belgium's neutrality. Fed on the teachings of imperialists and militants, Germans easily justified the breach of treaties as military necessities.

The plans of French strategists were heady. The disaster of 1870 and the fact that the army would be greatly outnumbered led planners to substitute offensive spirit and individual valor for the shortages of manpower. "Attack—always attack," the French soldier was told. Will power, guts, and sheer determination are what win battles. Plan Seventeen, therefore, provided that when the Germans drove westward the French armies to the south would head straight for Berlin, cut the Germans off, and destroy their armies piecemeal.

Russia planned a dual offensive, one against the Austrians north of the Carpathian Mountains, and the other against the German forces in East Prussia. Austria-Hungary was equally ambitious, proposing to subdue Serbia in a short campaign while pushing into Poland to defeat the Russians.

As for England, her weapon was to be the blockading and gradual strangulation of Germany from afar. Several years had passed since the French navy had taken over patrol of the Mediterranean, and the entire British fleet was massed at Scapa Flow, a base in the Orkney Islands, off Scotland.

Preceding pages: U.S. doughboys
man machine-gun post in quiet Vosges
sector in 1918.

A token force of six divisions was to join the French in land warfare.

On a June morning in 1914, a motorcade bearing the Archduke Francis Ferdinand, heir to the throne of Austria-Hungary, and his consort blundered into a wrong street in the sleepy Serbian town of Sarajevo. Before it could reverse its course, a consumptive young nationalist named Gavrilo Princip shot and killed them both. The case was a one-day sensation. During the next few weeks, however, Austria-Hungary determined to absorb Serbia once and for all. She obtained prompt assurances from the Kaiser and the German military command of "faithful support" in case Russia, Serbia's sponsor, made trouble.

Austria delivered a stiff ultimatum to Serbia and brusquely rejected the more than conciliatory reply. At the end of July, while panic swept the financial exchanges of the world, she declared war. Within the next five days the polarization of nations, which eventually caused fifty-seven of them to issue declarations of war against one another, proceeded with dizzying speed.

Mobilization of nearly six million men went into full swing, and reservists, their gun barrels stuffed with flowers, marched off to the accompaniment of wildly cheering crowds. On the evening of August 2, Germany issued an ultimatum to tiny Belgium. Give our troops passage through your country, it said in effect, or suffer the consequences. Albert, King of the Belgians, returned a ringing no, and for England, who felt her interests were inextricably bound up with the low-land countries, the die was cast. By August 4, all of the war declarations had been made, and in each country the joyful populace was being assured that their boys would be home before the first snowflake fell.

A good argument can be made that Germany lost the war in the first few weeks. Her reference to the treaty with Belgium as "a scrap of paper," her mass executions of Belgian civilian hostages, and the burning of entire towns alienated millions of neutrals around the world. Then, too, Germany amended and weakened the Schlieffen plan in ways that proved fatal. Holland was not included in the massive sweep; whole divisions were stripped from the right wing and sent to East Prussia, where Russia was moving faster than had

been expected; and finally the left-flank armies, which were supposed only to hold the line, took the offensive.

During the early days of fighting, however, the Germans seemed invincible. Only around Liége were the armies thrown off their six-week schedule for conquest, and then for just two days. As German troops goose-stepped through Brussels in never-ending streams, France launched the attacks that were to amputate the German forces in Belgium from the troops south of Sedan.

Plan Seventeen of the French quickly met total disaster. Élan and the will to win proved no match for massed German artillery and chattering machine guns. French infantry, conspicuous in scarlet and blue uniforms that had become a national tradition, were mowed down by the tens of thousands. By the fourth day it was all too clear that only retreat could spare the armies in northern France from a repetition of the catastrophe of 1870.

For ten days the French fell back to the Somme, the Aisne, and finally the Marne River. With them they carried the tiny British force which had acquitted itself well in its first encounter with the Germans along the banks of the Mons Canal. Only at the southern end of the line did the French defenses hold.

The guns of August had been firing for nearly a month and the German High Command convinced itself it was facing only the remnants of beaten armies which could be rounded up almost at will. General Alexander von Kluck, who was leading the weary German spearhead (his men had been marching twenty miles a day), suggested that the sweep not go forty miles west of Paris, as the Schlieffen plan dictated, but rather east of the city and push the defeated enemy back toward the borders of Germany. The fact that there might be French troops facing his right flank as the Germans streamed southward past Paris was dismissed as inconsequential. His plan was approved and, to the amazement of French reconnaissance patrols, the invading force wheeled sharply left.

There were troops to Kluck's right, a new army hastily thrown together by General Joseph Joffre, the French commander in chief, and entrusted to General Joseph Gallieni, a brilliant strategist. Gallieni instantly saw the possibilities of an attack on the German right flank.

What happened following Joffre's decision to end the retreat has become known as the Miracle of the Marne. Gallieni's regiments, which included 6,000 men rushed to the battlefield in Paris taxicabs, attacked along with hundreds of thousands of other supposedly defeated Frenchmen. Moltke, the German commander, nephew of the victorious field marshal of the Franco-Prussian War, was in trouble and called for a general retreat. The Germans fell back and dug in along the Aisne. For the next three months, the opposing forces edged northward in a so-called race for the channel ports that ended in a deadlock when the British held off a desperate German attempt to end the war quickly at Ypres. Meanwhile, the aggressiveness of the Russians caused the Germans to rush divisions from France to the eastern front and eased the pressure on the Allies in the West.

Tsar Nicholas II, the Little Father to whom an overwhelming majority of Russians rallied at the outbreak of hostilities, was one of history's least admirable rulers, smug, prejudiced, and monumentally stupid. His closest advisers were, for the most part, corrupt, incompetent, and empty-headed autocrats, often with violent pro-German sympathies. Although some efforts had been made to reshape the army after the Japanese debacle, most of the generals in command were superannuated numskulls. As a result, the Russian soldier, stolid, brave, and able to withstand incredible adversity, went off to war under miserable conditions—often without a rifle or the cartridges for it, without food, shells, or boots.

In mid-August of 1914, in response to frantic pleas from France for help, Russian troops crossed the German border. The capture of a few East Prussian towns caused panic in Berlin and led to the appointment of Generals Paul von Hindenburg and Erich Ludendorff to the eastern command.

Two Russian armies were supposed to march in concert and close on the Germans in a pincers movement. To make a complicated story short, the commanding general of one, who had become an enemy of the commanding general of the other as the result of a squabble years before, suddenly stopped his advance while his colleague kept moving. Spotting an opportunity to destroy the Russian armies separately, the Germans attacked, surrounded, and annihilated one army in the Battle of Tannenberg, taking more than 90,000 prisoners.

Then, turning on the other, they drove it eastward in wild disorder. While the rout was partly compensated for by an impressive victory over the Austrians in Silesia, the tragedy of Tannenberg added to a growing spirit of defeatism throughout Russia.

Once the vast opening battles of 1914 ended, the war settled down to a bloody stalemate. On the western front, six hundred miles of trenches zigzagged southward across French soil, from the English Channel to the Swiss border, and millions of men, living in mud, blood, and filth, faced one another across a no man's land interlaced with barbed wire. At intervals, almost as though they were planned as massive instruments of self-destruction, one side or the other launched offensives that were supposed to break the deadlock and lead to a resumption of a war of movement. Each resulted in pathetic gains of a few hundred yards, or a mile or so, along tiny salients with losses running into hundreds of thousands. From 1915 to 1917, with each seeking the illusory breakthrough, Germany introduced poison gas, the British the tank, while both sides perfected the art of mass artillery barrages of undreamed-of proportions. Only in the skies above the trenches was the war personalized, as the airplane came into its own and a succession of dogfights in Fokkers, Nieuports, and Spads made heroes of men such as Richthofen, Fonck, Guynemer, and Ball, almost all of whom met their death before the fighting ended.

On the home fronts the big jobs were the making of munitions and the production and training of human fodder for the guns. Great Britain, which never planned to engage in land warfare on a large scale, was bled white as it raised huge armies throughout England and the empire. In Flanders, Champagne, Artois, and along the Somme, Allied offensives were launched on high notes of optimism and ended with insignificant gains and casualty lists of horrifying proportions. Only the huge German offensive at Verdun in 1916 came close to a breakthrough, but the French held their positions, and after four months of hell all the German mincing machine had to show for its effort was nearly 600,000 dead and wounded.

On other fronts the fighting was slightly more conclusive. Russia continued to launch offensives with diminishing enthusiasm, generally with success against the Austrians but none at all where Germany was concerned. Japan entered the war early and contented herself with seizing the German colony of Kiaochow on the Chinese mainland and island possessions in the Pacific, all of which proved costly settings for World War II.

After two years of frustration, General Jan Christian Smuts' South African troops finally took over the last German colonies in Africa. Turkey and Bulgaria threw in their lot with the Central Powers, and the Allies ran up frightful casualty lists fighting Turks and Germans in the Near East and in abortive landings on the Gallipoli Peninsula. Serbia, after fighting bravely, was crushed in 1915, and Rumania, which joined the Allied cause in 1916, was overwhelmed and occupied by Germany. Italy, after carefully weighing the offers made by both sides, entered on the Allied side early in 1915. Although her troops fought bravely, nearly a million Italians became victims of no less than ten successive offensives through the howling wilderness of the Carso, the rocky, barren country near the Austrian frontier. Weakened by endless repulses, the Italians became easy victims for the Austro-German offensive in 1917 and would have been knocked out of the war after a disaster at Caporetto had not French and English divisions rushed to their aid.

The great surprise of the war on the high seas was the behavior of Germany's powerful fleet which, like Sherlock Holmes's dog in the night, did nothing. Only once, in the spring of 1916, did it venture forth from its anchorage to test British supremacy in the Battle of Jutland. Although it doled out more punishment than it received, it slipped back to harbor for the duration of the war. Instead of head-to-head fighting with capital ships, the Germans elected to turn to submarine warfare. Early in 1915 she announced that any merchant ship in the waters surrounding Great Britain would be liable to attack, and followed up the threat by sinking the British liner *Lusitania.* More than a thousand lives were lost, among them 127 Americans. Although the Germans claimed (almost certainly correctly) that the ship was carrying arms and ammunition to be used against her, the reaction of the United States was so violent that the Germans backed down and agreed to Woodrow Wilson's demand for the limitation of submarine warfare, a promise she kept for more than a year, until (as many experts maintain) she had built enough new

undersea boats to imperil England's survival.

In the last months of 1916 it became obvious that Russia was near collapse, but when Tsar Nicholas was urged to make an effort to regain the confidence of his people, he said, "Do you mean that I am to regain the confidence of my people or that they are to regain mine?"

Incredibly, Russia fought on for another year. But after the collapse of the summer offensive of 1917, the exhausted nation fell like a ripe plum into the hands of Lenin and the Bolsheviks. With Russia out of the war, Germany was free to send more than a million additional men to the western front.

The German High Command knew very well that there was need for speed, since troops from the United States were arriving in France in growing numbers. America's entry had come less than five months after Woodrow Wilson had squeaked through his re-election on the slogan, "He kept us out of the war."

There were major reasons for Wilson's abrupt change from "There is such a thing as being too proud to fight" to battling to "Make the world safe for democracy." First, in early 1917, Hindenburg and his associates convinced the Kaiser that Germany's only hope of victory rested on starving Great Britain through the resumption of unrestricted submarine warfare; as the number of sinkings increased, American indignation rose. Second, the British intercepted a note from German Foreign Minister Zimmermann to his representative in Mexico, offering to reconquer in Mexico's behalf "the lost territory in Texas, New Mexico, and Arizona" if Mexico would support Germany in the event of war with the United States. America was outraged. Woodrow Wilson, despite deep misgivings, asked for a declaration of war and got a tumultuous ovation from Congress. "My message today," Wilson was quoted as saying that night, "was a message of death for our young men. How strange it seems to applaud that." Then Wilson laid his head on a table and wept.

By the end of 1917, British and American convoys that had gone into operation in May, when German sinkings of Allied shipping reached a point of near disaster for Great Britain, succeeded in overcoming the U-boat peril. Thirty-one submarines were destroyed in the last four months of the year, a rate far beyond Germany's replacement capacity.

In the spring and summer of 1918, reinforced by troops and guns from the silent eastern front, the Germans made their last desperate bid for victory. A series of offensives brought the Kaiser's forces closer to a breakthrough than at any time since 1914. The first two, aimed at the British, were finally stopped at Armentières and Amiens. Most dangerous of all was a drive along the Aisne River, where five German divisions smashed through the Allied center and headed for Paris. In the second battle of the Marne, American divisions at Château-Thierry, Belleau Wood, and Cantigny went into battle for the first time and helped stop the German advance.

In early August, after the last German attacks sputtered to a halt, the Allies went over to the offensive. On the eighth of the month, which Ludendorff called the "blackest day in the history of the German Army," French troops gained up to seven miles and for the first time found German troops fleeing in panic before them. The advance continued and by the end of the month Ludendorff, who for two years had made virtually all of Germany's decisions as Wilhelm faded into obscurity, notified his commanders that an armistice was Germany's only chance to avoid invasion and disaster. There followed an adroit move to shift the blame for defeat from the army's shoulders. Prince Max of Baden, a liberal, was given the chancellorship and appealed for an armistice on the basis of Woodrow Wilson's Fourteen Points. It was this move that gave rise to the legend that came to be widely believed in later years: The German army was never defeated; it was stabbed in the back by democrats and defeatists.

The fighting dragged on, attended by the collapse and surrender of Germany's partners on other fronts. By the end of October the Allied armies had reached or crossed prewar borders and were poised for invasion of Germany. Ludendorff quit, German sailors at Kiel mutinied, and Germany became a republic with Fritz Ebert, a Socialist, as chancellor. The Kaiser, after some vague talk about dying with his troops, thought better of it and fled to refuge in Holland. The next day, in the predawn gloom of November 11, the Germans signed an armistice document that amounted to unconditional surrender.

The costs of the Great War were staggering. Nearly sixty percent of the 65,000,000 men who were put into uniform became casualties. Nearly 9,000,000 died. Russia, with nearly 7,000,000 dead and wounded, had the highest count. German casualties reached 6,000,000, while those of France topped 5,500,000—more than one-fourth her prewar male population. The British Empire mourned nearly 1,000,000 dead and 2,000,000 wounded.

The note of high idealism sounded in Woodrow Wilson's Fourteen Points—no secret diplomacy, removal of economic barriers, mutual guarantees of political independence, and the rest of them—faded when the victors gathered at Versailles to make peace. Wilson made compromise after compromise to bring into being his cherished hope for a League of Nations, which in action proved inept and ineffectual. Gradually the victorious survivors forgot about making the world safe for democracy and switched to a mood of *never again*.

This German postcard sentiment
typifies euphoria with which Europe
entered the war in 1914.

MUSÉE DE LA GUERRE / AMERICAN HERITAGE

Opposite: German and Austrian soldiers
aboard tender in Lemberg (Lvov) area of Poland,
1915, probably en route to eastern front
to smash Russians. Left: Under fire,
French machine-gunner sprints for shelter.
Bottom: German horde advances, somewhere
in France, early in war.

"Furnace of Verdun," 1916: French infantry marching up to narrow front where Germans had launched terrible war of attrition. Eventually, ten months of slaughter cost France and Germany 900,000 men killed, wounded, or taken prisoner.

Moment of Death: French *poilu* (center) is shot in mid-stride during small-scale action against German trench in Champagne area, 1917. Following pages: French bury German dead in trench. French machine-gunners of 1914, before it was decided —reluctantly—to issue steel helmets.

99

Munitions workers (above) making artillery
shells in England. British gun crew (opposite)
—in cloth regimental caps—prepares to
fire a round somewhere on western front, 1915.
Inferiority of British ammunition and
number of duds produced created a scandal
in early years of the war.

British officer leads Tommies "over the top" on first day of Somme offensive in 1916. Two of 60,000 casualties Britain suffered that day can be seen at right in sequence below. Somme was British Verdun, a slaughter that gained inches and eventually cost 1,250,000 British, French, and German casualties.

Terror at Sea: Submarine warfare against supply
ships was German effort to starve Britain out of war.
Having torpedoed victim, U-boat often surfaced
(below), while stunned survivors flocked
to overloaded lifeboats. Stricken ship (opposite)
plunges to bottom. Note man at top still
clinging to lifeline.

U.S. BUREAU OF SHIPS ▲

U.S. SIGNAL CORPS

59

Lafayette Escadrille, American volunteers
flying for France, poses outside hangar at Toul in
1918, with ground crewmen and Type XIII
Spads bearing well-known Indian-head
insignia. Air war was primitive, but chivalrous,
and grew in importance as conflict wore on.

E-4924

17781

Breguet 14 (opposite) was a French bomber also used by Americans in last year of war. Bomb racks under wing (like those below), rear cockpit with swiveling guns for gunner, and forward machine gun synchronized to fire through whirling propeller were World War I innovations. Bottom: Pranged German Albatross.

Above: Canadians on way to victory
over Germans at Vimy Ridge, 1915. Opposite:
Ammunition and supplies for American
advance through Argonne in 1918.

Opposite: U.S. casualties from first
day of Meuse-Argonne offensive
crowd field hospital located in
ruined church of Neuville.
Above: Battle fatigue, 1918.

RUSSIAN REVOL

On the day after the coronation of Nicholas II in 1896, a rush for free gifts at a celebration of the event in Moscow got out of hand. In the stampede that followed, more than 1,300 men, women, and children were crushed to death.

The tragedy proved an augury of a reign punctuated by disaster: crop failures, economic depressions, industrial strife, peasant unrest, pogroms, senseless terrorism, an unpopular conflict with the Japanese that wound up in ignominious defeat, and a popular but lethal war that ended with the overthrow of the Romanovs and the execution of the Tsar and all his family.

A fatalist at heart, Nicholas took each catastrophe in stride. He had been born, ironically, on the Feast of Job and liked to quote the unhappy prophet: "Hardly do I have a fear than it is realized, and all the misfortunes that I dread fall on me." Nicholas's real problems were a shallow mind and a blind distaste for reform and all democratic processes.

The greatest disaster of all was Nicholas's beloved wife, the Tsarina Alexandra. Originally Princess Alice of Hesse-Darmstadt, a granddaughter of Queen Victoria, she changed her name and converted to Orthodox Catholicism before her marriage. Alexandra was tense, neurotic, and humorless. Her depth of religious feelings was paralleled only by her dedication to mysticism and quackery in all its forms—harmless enough, perhaps, until they led her to meddle in affairs of state. In short order she became the hated "German woman" to millions of Russians. When Alexandra's only son Alexei (born after four daughters) was found to be an incurable hemophiliac on whom the smallest scratch might induce a fatal hemorrhage, her mental state thereafter verged on hysteria, a condition that abated only when the miracle she prayed for was granted.

"We have got to know a man of God, Grigori, from the Tobolsk region," Nicholas wrote in his diary in 1905. The miracle was Grigori Rasputin, a grotesque unordained monk. "Rasputin" means "the debauched," and the unkempt and lecherous *starets* lived up to his name. Alexandra, however, soon came to believe that only Rasputin could prolong the life of her son and passionately defended him against all criticism. The consequences proved disastrous.

For more than a century, periods of reform in Russia had alternated with merciless repression. Unhappily such changes as the emancipation of the serfs and an improved school system did little to better the economic welfare of the peasants or factory workers. These were the Dark People, the faceless and voteless human herd whose mute but vaguely menacing presence disturbed the sleep of Russian autocrats.

At the other end of the scale was the highly vocal intelligentsia, ranging from nihilists and terrorists who lived and died by the gun and the bomb, to writers like Pushkin and Turgenev, most of whom believed that the answers to Russia's problem lay not in a violent overthrow of the government but a gradual conversion to the British system of liberal, constitutional rule.

Radical groups who plotted violent revolution were badly divided among themselves. Some felt it would come through peasant uprisings. Others held with Marx that workers would rise up to create a new society, although Marx expected that world revolution would begin in a more highly industrialized state like Germany. Still a third splinter group, the Bolsheviks, felt that the revolution would be made by a small, hard-core group of dedicated activists, leaders of the herd, so to speak, who would drive the stampede toward Marxist goals.

The outbreak of war in 1914 made revolution seem further away than ever. As waves of patriotic fervor swept Russia, Nicholas found himself suddenly popular. Before a vast throng in St. Petersburg (soon changed to the less Germanic Petrograd), he solemnly repeated the oath Alexander I took when Napoleon invaded Russia a century earlier: no peace so long as a single enemy soldier remained on the soil of the motherland.

The national mood, amounting almost to exultation, faded when the military disaster at Tannenberg ended all hope of a victorious invasion of Germany. Early Russian gains against the Austrians were wiped out, and in 1915 the Kaiser's divisions overran Lithuania and most of Poland. Russian casualties were hideous—more than 4,000,000 —and the supply problem became a national disgrace. Companies were sent into battle with one rifle for every two, three, or five men. There was a shortage of big guns and shells for them. There were shortages of food, transport, and fodder for horses at the front, and a scarcity of almost everything at home.

Nicholas, increasingly irritated by criticism from the Duma and by gossip about Rasputin and the Tsarina, decided to take overall command of the armies himself. Until then they had been led by his uncle, the Grand Duke Nicholas, a well-meaning giant of a man who didn't disguise his feelings about Rasputin. When the monk expressed an intention of visiting the troops, the Grand Duke replied, "Come and I'll hang you." Naturally, the Tsarina pressed the Tsar hard to remove the Grand Duke. He was getting too popular, she said, and was planning to depose Nicholas. The Tsar vacillated and finally gave way. The Grand Duke was shunted to the Caucasus, and Nicholas departed for army headquarters at Mogilev.

In the Tsar's absence, Rasputin became virtual ruler of Russia. Each day he announced his decisions to the Tsarina who, in turn, relayed them, in the form of commands, to the absent Tsar. "Get rid of Polivanov," she would write, referring to the new liberal minister of war. And then, a few days later, "Lovey, don't dawdle."

Before long twenty-one ministers, many of them capable, were dismissed and their places taken by charlatans and traitors and the husbands of women who slept with Rasputin. As the travesty continued, the Tsarina's letters to Nicholas became more strident. "Russia loves to feel the whip. . . . How I wish I could pour my will into your veins." And again, "Crush them all under you. . . . We have been placed by God on the throne and we must keep it firm and give it over to our son untouched."

Soldiers began to desert by the thousands, strikes and bread lines grew longer, and a sense of apathy and despair spread through Russia during the bitter winter of 1916. As the New Year approached, a group of young aristocrats murdered Rasputin, but his death came too late to make a difference. The grief-stricken Tsarina carried on as before, and Nicholas, when warned that revolution was imminent, returned to army headquarters. "I shall take up dominoes in my spare time," he said.

The revolution, which began in Petrograd, crept rather than burst on the world. On March 8, striking workers looted bakeries. The next day the street mobs were large, left-wing radicals began to take an interest in what was going on, and for the first time Cossacks, who had been ordered to charge the crowds, disobeyed the command. Soldiers were beginning to fraternize with the mob.

Frantic messages went to Nicholas. "I order that disorders in the capital shall be stopped tomorrow," he commanded placidly. It was like trying to sop up the ocean with a pocket handkerchief. Things soon were entirely out of hand. Regiment after regiment of the Petrograd garrison mutinied and joined the mobs attacking police stations and looting stores. Nicholas finally decided to return to Petrograd, but his train was halted by railway workers and forced to turn back. On March 15, in the same mood of resignation with which he accepted other tragedies in his life, he abdicated.

Out of the vacuum created by the remarkably bloodless revolution came the middle-of-the-road provisional government headed by a glib and persuasive lawyer named Alexander Kerensky. Buoyed by Allied loans, and a Duma that for the first time was something more than a debating society, most Russians were in favor of carrying on the war.

When news of the uprisings in Petrograd reached Lenin in Zurich, he was skeptical. Even the abdication of the Tsar failed to convince him that the time was ripe for his kind of revolution. After several weeks of unrest and turmoil, however, Lenin and other radical exiles began to feel that it might be the real thing after all and contacted the German minister in Switzerland on ways and means of getting to their homeland. Convinced that transporting Lenin and the other peace-at-any-price radicals to Petrograd was the best answer to its problem, the German government offered a train to the exiles.

And so, "like a plague bacillus," as Winston Churchill put it, Lenin, plus thirty-one others, made his historic arrival at the Finland Station. He had expected hostility and possible arrest. Instead, there were bands and Bolshevik slogans and flowery speeches.

Lenin listened impatiently to the oratory and then brought his followers up sharply. It wasn't what they expected or wanted to hear: the world-wide revolution had come, the Petrograd Soviet was a stooge of the bourgeoisie, the Provisional Government must be destroyed, no compromise with any other party. And on and on, leaving the party members feeling as though they had "been beaten about the head that night with flails."

Lenin's triumph, however, did not come until six months later. With Kerensky in the post of war minister, a new offensive against the Germans was launched in late June. For two weeks it made progress and then the counterattack began. Another crushing Russian defeat quickly resulted.

As news of the setback reached Petrograd, fresh street disturbances broke out, organized (historians are virtually certain) by the Bolsheviks and German agents in the city. More than 400 people were killed and wounded before a summer rain squall helped to dampen the ardor of the mob. When calm was restored, the government issued a document that purported to show Lenin was a German agent and that the Bolsheviks had created the uprising to coincide with the German attacks. In the wave of bitterness that followed, Lenin fled to Finland, while Trotsky and other Bolshevik leaders were arrested.

For another six or seven weeks, Lenin's fortunes remained at low ebb. He himself expected at any moment to be apprehended and shot. Then the Bolsheviks had a stroke of great good luck. The recently appointed army chief, convinced that Russia needed a strong man at the helm, decided to seize power by military coup d'état. It fizzled. Workers struck, the troops refused to march, the general was carted off to prison, and Kerensky clung to the increasingly shaky helm of the ship of state. But a wave of leftist sentiment swept the country and average citizens said, in effect, "Suppose Lenin *was* in the pay of the Germans? Kerensky and his gang are being paid by the Americans and French and English. And the war, the damned war, goes on and on."

In late October a bewigged and clean-shaven Lenin slipped into Petrograd and met with Trotsky, Stalin, and nine other members of his inner circle. By three in the morning the group agreed that an immediate armed uprising was imperative. What John Reed called "Ten Days That Shook the World" followed. The Bolsheviks made no secret of their plans. Lenin proclaimed them on November 1, when he wrote for the newspapers, "The famine will not wait . . . the war will not wait."

The fate of Russia from 1917 to the present day was settled in the heart of Petrograd over a single issue: control of the armed forces in and around that city. Bolshevik headquarters were in a girls' school, the Smolny Institute. Kerensky and his increasingly indecisive followers made wishy-washy stabs at suppressing the uprising from the Winter Palace. In the last analysis, probably the strongest weapons in the Bolshevik arsenal were the brilliant and inflammatory speeches of Trotsky to segments of the Petrograd garrison.

The Cossacks looked the other way as armed Red Guards took over in the streets. Trainloads of rebellious sailors arrived from Kronstadt naval station. Regiments of the city's garrison either supported the Bolsheviks or remained neutral—and Kerensky left the city in a desperate attempt to round up reinforcements for his cause. While he was gone the city was irrevocably lost and Lenin stood listening to the thunderous ovation of his followers in Smolny. When the noise died down, he said simply, "We shall now proceed to construct the Socialist order." And so he did. Kerensky fled the country after an attempt to regain power failed because of Cossack desertions. Gradually, vast stretches of Russia were won over, as Trotsky put it, by telegraph.

Before the Bolshevik regime became firmly entrenched, however, it was obliged to survive three brushes with disaster. First, the election that was held throughout Russia to elect a constituent assembly gave Lenin and his followers less than 10,000,000 votes; his opponents polled 42,000,000. Lenin and Trotsky solved this problem by seeing to it that Bolshevik troops broke up the first meeting of the assembly. Then, when Lenin made good on his promise to seek peace with Germany, he was obliged to tell his people that the terms forced on him amounted to a partition of Russia. Under the terms of the treaty signed at Brest Litovsk early in 1918, more than 1,300,000 square miles of territory were given up, an area with a population of 62,000,000 Russians which contained three-quarters of her coal and iron resources.

Finally, the Communists (the name had just been changed from Social Democrats Workers' Party) were obliged to fend off the advances of White armies, composed of right-of-center factions, that were closing in from all sides. In overcoming this danger, Trotsky sensed that the original Bolshevik concept of supplanting a regular army with worker militias and Red Guards wasn't going to work. He quickly introduced conscription and, with 50,000 former tsarist officers in charge, built the Communist forces to a peak of 5,000,000 men.

The death of the royal family was a by-product of the effort of the White armies to gain control. Following Nicholas's abdication, efforts to export the Romanovs to England collapsed and they were subsequently moved from Petrograd to Ekaterinburg (now Sverdlovsk) in the Urals. Here they were treated with an ascending degree of hostility. On July 16, 1918, at a time when the anti-Communist Czech Legion was nearing the town, they were taken to the cellar of the house that had been their prison and exterminated. Virtually no announcement was made at the time to the Russian people, but later twenty-eight of the murderers were arrested and five of them executed.

The Civil War dragged on for two more years as the White forces were defeated one after another. The last formal attempt to oust the Red regime ended in October, 1920, when the army of Baron Peter Wrangel was routed attempting to cross the Dnieper in its drive northward.

Lenin, victimized by a series of strokes, lived out his last few years watching helplessly and with growing concern as the power struggle he feared developed between Trotsky and the man of whom he had said, "Comrade Stalin . . . has concentrated enormous power in his hands, and I am not sure that he always knows how to use that power with sufficient caution."

Opposite: Revolution began with mild street demonstrations in Petrograd. Below: Once imperial troops and Cossacks fraternized with demonstrators, Romanov dynasty quickly toppled, and street fighting like this was sporadic.
Right: Moscow scene, 1917.

Opposite: Imperial soldiers, red
flags flying from their bayonets, joined
revolution in April, 1917. Top:
Soldiers and civilians attack
Winter Palace in Petrograd.
Bottom: Demonstration in front of
Petrograd opera house.

Right: After last Russian offensive in Poland, in late summer of 1917, Kerensky Government collapsed and troops like these deserted in vast numbers. Note that many men have discarded their rifles. Below: Soldiers raise red flag at Kremlin after abdication of the Tsar. Following pages: Students and Red soldiers and sailors battle police in streets of Petrograd.

CULVER PICTURES

SPANISH CIVIL

WAR 1936-1939

Spain is a land of violent contrasts. The great central plain, girdled by mountains, is bitterly cold in winter and monstrously hot in summer. His country, a Spaniard will tell you, has nine months of winter and three months of hell. Nearly half the land is barren, yet in some regions the soil is incredibly rich. Record-breaking rainfalls are matched by record-breaking droughts.

In a country where the unexpected is the rule rather than the exception, it was no great surprise when Spain became a republic in the early 1930s, as Europe and most of the world was swinging toward totalitarianism—Fascist, Communist, or Nazi. As the world depression deepened in 1930, Primo de Rivera resigned as dictator of Spain after more than seven years of what he described as "continuous uneasiness, responsibility and labor." It had been a typical strong-arm regime, its repressiveness camouflaged by his vitality, humor, and intelligence. Once he was gone, however, Alfonso XIII was unable to cope with Spain's problems; he abdicated and left the country. Without bloodshed the first democratic regime took over.

The mild beginning was deceptive. The moment Alfonso was gone and the first President elected, Spain's problems proliferated. In an excess of enthusiasm, the legislature disestablished the Catholic Church and forbade religious orders to teach. Divorce was permitted and women were given the vote. While the motives of the reformers were laudable—to keep the Church out of government, to wipe out illiteracy, to give unworked lands owned by indifferent aristocrats to hungry peasants—the effects of these measures were catastrophic. Spanish women were violently conservative and pro-Church. And when the Church schools were closed down, it developed that there were no schools at all for seventy-five percent of Spain's children.

During the four years of chaos and escalating dissatisfaction that ensued, two Spains emerged—the new and the old. Twenty-eight governments rose and fell and reactionary regimes succeeded leftist coalitions. Meanwhile, as a gradual polarization to the extreme right and left took place, the Spanish scene was illuminated by violence and terrorism. Murders and bombings, riots and shootings, church burnings and minor insurrections became daily happenings as the fast-growing

Fascist party, the Falange, matched and outdid the tactics of its socialist, liberal, and Communist enemies.

The Spanish Civil War, one of the bloodiest fratricidal conflicts in history, erupted in the summer of 1936 and lasted for nearly three years. When it ended, more than a million Spaniards had died and much of the country was in ruins. It began when the Popular Front government, under the leadership of Largo Caballero, swung sharply to the left. The Spanish army in Morocco revolted and nearly every garrison in the country immediately followed suit.

The Nationalists, as the rebels were called, had the support of a number of hitherto antagonistic groups: Carlists who wanted a return to monarchy, Falangists who were anticlerical and antimonarchist, the Church, the nobility, wealthy landowners, industrialists, as well as a large segment of the bourgeoisie. Allied against them were the Loyalists, groups that fought continuously among themselves—workers, intellectuals, part of the peasantry, militant Communists, liberals, and (surprisingly) most of the Spanish naval and air forces.

The war quickly became a testing ground for the world conflict that was waiting in the wings. Fascist Italy poured 50,000 troops and Nazi Germany dispatched 10,000 airmen and specialists to aid the army of General Francisco Franco. Both nations supplied tanks, planes, and artillery, while Stalin's Russia shipped to the Republican Loyalists all of these plus hundreds of technical advisors to maintain discipline among the Communists who had entered Spain from many countries to help the Loyalist cause.

Outstanding was the International Brigade, whose ranks included a great many dedicated liberals—among them George Orwell and Ernest Hemingway. It was primarily a Communist enterprise, a fact that eventually led to the disillusionment of some of the concerned idealists who enlisted under its banner. As for the great democracies, most of them sympathized with the Loyalist cause but maintained a hands-off attitude.

Most military experts assumed that the Nationalist army would crush the Loyalists in short order, but because its troops were poorly trained and equipped it soon lost control of Barcelona, Madrid, and most of the leading manufacturing centers of the industrial north. As the fighting

Preceding pages: International Brigade encampment, winter campaign, 1936.

progressed, formal fronts came into existence. The most important was Madrid, where for three years the Loyalist troops —workers, clerks, schoolteachers, lawyers, students, and artists —repulsed attacks by Nationalist forces beyond its walls and a fifth column of undercover Nationalists within its gates.

For a time it looked as though the Loyalists might win. Italian troops were routed at Guadalajara, the Loyalists gained considerable territory, and German bombers stiffened Republican backs when they staged the senseless and destructive bombing of Guernica. But as 1938 wore on, the overwhelming strength of the Nationalists began to take effect. Franco, a man of no particular political conviction except for his traditional belief in law and order, curbed the bloody leanings of the Falangists, erased discord among his quarrelsome followers, and managed to create a viable economy in the areas he had conquered. Without such leadership, the Loyalists continued to fight among themselves and Russian aid stopped. Barcelona fell to Franco's army and two months later Madrid unconditionally surrendered.

In the years that followed, all the trappings of dictatorship were restored. The divorce law was repealed, religious education was brought back, and the privileges of wealthy landowners were reinforced. Censorship and repression became the order of the day, Nevertheless, Spain proved once more her talent for the unexpected. In October, 1940, Adolf Hitler arrived in his special train at the town of Hendaye on the Franco-Spanish border. France had fallen and Great Britain stood alone, facing the invincible Nazi colossus. Hitler's goal was simple: Spain had made a pact with Germany and under its terms he asked Franco to take over Gibraltar from the dying British lion. To Hitler's amazement, Franco refused. Long hours of wrangling got the *Führer* nowhere. "Rather than go through that again, I would have three or four teeth yanked out," he said to Mussolini. Nonetheless, Hitler did try again in 1941. "Only in the case of our victory," he wrote Franco in urging him to seize Gibraltar, "will your present regime continue to exist." Once more Franco refused, and Hitler finally gave up.

Despite Hitler's prediction, El Caudillo's regime has endured. For more than thirty-five years, Franco has walked a tightrope, clapping the lid down quickly on rightists and leftists alike who threatened to step out of line. On occasions he has defied the Church, slapped down his Falangist supporters, and maintained equilibrium in the face of a vast assortment of difficulties. What happens when he dies and Prince Juan Carlos (Franco's choice as successor) brings back monarchy to Spain is anybody's guess. One reasonably safe hypothesis is that whatever happens will be unexpected. That is the Spanish way.

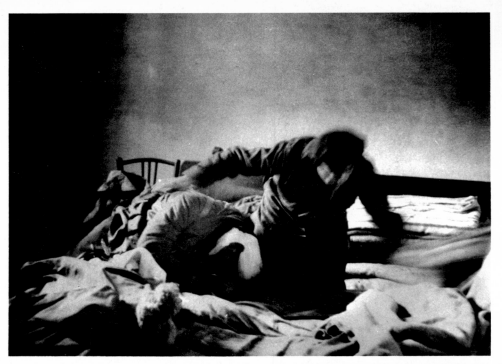

Opposite: Wounded defender of Madrid (top).
Department-store employees running for shelter
as air-raid alert is sounded in Bilbao (bottom).
Below: Besieged citizens of Madrid watch
as Loyalist planes—off-camera—attack Junker
bombers which had been devastating city.

Dispossessed: Young refugee (above),
old woman and child (opposite), who fled Malaga
as Franco's troops approached.

Opposite: Luggage commandeered from nearby railroad station is used for barricade in fighting for Madrid (top). Basques defending Bilbao (middle). Bottom: "And the fine hope," Capa wrote, "more often than not ends like this." Below: Levering a field piece into position in muddy ground on plains surrounding Madrid.

French gendarme leads defeated Loyalists across border after fall of Barcelona. As war came to an end, some 400,000 refugees —civilians and soldiers—sought shelter in France, whose own day of reckoning with Fascist powers was less than a year away.

CHINESE CIVIL

WAR 1919-1949

The painful birth of modern China, a country roughly the area of the United States, that crowds within its borders one fifth of the human race, may well be the most important event of this century. To the western mind the story of that birth is as hard to understand as the Chinese habit of moving the head from side to side to denote "yes" and nodding it up and down to signify "no."

In truth, the Chinese revolution was not a revolution at all. It was thirty-eight years of local insurrections and civil war, of regional blood baths and piratical incursions. Simultaneously, it was a succession of less than wholehearted efforts to fend off a rapacious Japan, which pillaged and despoiled the land and the people.

Until Great Britain established the first western colony in China at Hong Kong early in the nineteenth century, China at times came close to being the peaceable kingdom of man's dream. For twenty-two centuries, emperors, each the Son of Heaven, had ruled their subjects, generally with restraint and often with a considerable measure of democracy. One language and one religion had lasted for an even longer period. "What you do not like when done to yourself, do not do unto others," Confucius taught five hundred years before the birth of Christ. Filial piety is the basis of virtue and the origin of culture, he said, and on this base a towering edifice of ancestor worship was erected. It was a humane philosophy, but one that preserved the status quo at the expense of innovation and mental exploration. As a result, China entered the twentieth century ill-equipped to survive in a world that had been industrialized and toughened in the crucible of competitive warfare.

Western businessmen and missionaries who poured into China before 1900 were initially greeted with tolerance and a mild degree of complacency. But as one foreign nation after another began forcibly to wring trading concessions and prime operating bases from the Chinese empire, resentment spread through the land. Business ventures established by the foreigners made profits of a hundred or more percent a year, while Chinese laborers grew progressively poorer, working twelve to sixteen hours a day for salaries ranging from three to fourteen cents. Further resentment was caused by the patronizing approach of some of the missionaries, but their teachings did succeed in tearing gaping holes in China's intellectual wall.

A growing number of Chinese students began to attend western schools where they picked up ideas directly opposed to the traditional Manchu way of doing things.

China's frustration deepened in 1894, when Japan, having learned that the meek do not inherit the earth, crushed the army of the Dowager Empress Tzu Hsi in a brief war. Six years later, Chinese hatred of foreign exploiters erupted in the Boxer Rebellion, an uprising ruthlessly suppressed by troops from assorted western nations.

Following the Boxer insurrection, Tzu Hsi, a canny, ambitious, and once-beautiful woman who began her career as an imperial concubine, instituted a series of reforms. A constitution was promised, western courses were introduced into school curricula and the classical examination system, which had been used for twenty-one hundred years, was abolished.

The old Empress, who had ruled China for more than four decades, didn't move fast enough to satisfy the bitter young radicals who cut off their queues to signify defiance of the Manchu regime. Their leader was Dr. Sun Yat-sen, whose schooling in Honolulu and subsequent western medical training in Hong Kong had converted him to Anglican Christianity and democratic processes. Beginning in 1895, Sun Yat-sen divided his time between fund-raising trips to various parts of the globe and directing more than a half-dozen abortive uprisings. Finally, when a weak regency followed the death of the Empress, the military revolted and overthrew the Manchu dynasty, which had ruled for more than two centuries. In one of history's more ironic moments, Sun Yat-sen turned the presidency of the new republic over to Yuan Shih-kai, the strong man who commanded the opposing Imperial Army. Dr. Sun believed that it was the only way to avoid civil war and to work out his "Three Principles of the People"—the expulsion of foreigners from privileged positions, the establishment of true democracy, and the redistribution of land held by greedy landlords to the peasants.

Yuan's brief regime was a disaster. Japan had entered World War I on the side of the Allies and, conscious that her partners would not attempt to thwart her ambitions, made a series of outrageous demands on China designed to give Japan administrative and economic control. Yuan temporized,

Preceding pages:
Nationalist troops on maneuvers.
Coal-scuttle helmets place picture before
U.S. entry into war, when China had
German advisers and equipment.
Most Chinese units were far more
threadbare than this one.

gave way to some of the demands, but then briefly declared himself emperor. His own generals joined in the outcry against this move and a revolt began. Yuan hastily reversed himself and soon afterward died of "disease and chagrin."

From 1916 to 1925 chaos reigned, a state that well suited the Japanese, who gradually extended their foothold. In 1919 the former German naval base of Tsingtao was taken over through a secret deal concocted by the victorious Allies without China's knowledge, and student riots protesting the deal were crushed. Frustration and despair—and with them, hatred of the foreigners—mounted.

During this era Peking was nominally the capital of the country, and to that sprawling city came an endless procession of puppet governments, each installed by whatever war lord happened to be victorious at the moment. Meanwhile, in southern China, Sun Yat-sen attempted to maintain a "legal" republican government in Canton. His party, the Kuomintang, became the rallying point for all the left-of-center splinter groups. One of Sun's aides was a Moscow-trained and somewhat enigmatic young man named Chiang Kai-shek, who combined revolutionary tendencies with a surprising affinity for merchants and bankers in Shanghai and the secret societies that controlled Chinese labor.

As the Kuomintang grew, Sun Yat-sen asked the western powers for recognition and financial aid. He was turned down and when they stubbornly gave support to each succeeding corrupt regime in Peking, Sun Yat-sen turned to Russia. Moscow not only recognized the Kuomintang but promptly sent political and military advisors.

The Chinese Communist party came into being in 1921, when thirteen young men, among them Mao Tse-tung, organized a cell; at about the same time a group of students in Paris, one of whom was Chou En-lai, followed suit. As the movement spread, its members individually joined the Kuomintang.

Sun Yat-sen died in 1925 and a few weeks later eleven students who were protesting the suppression of a textile strike in Shanghai were gunned down by the private police force maintained by the foreign residents of the International Settlement. More than any other event, this act poured fresh fuel on Chinese hatred of foreigners and kept the Kuomin-

tang functioning after Sun's death. Trained and reorganized by Russian military advisors and led by Chiang Kai-shek, the new Nationalist army of the Kuomintang swept to a string of quick victories over the war lords. Nanking fell and Kuomintang soldiers rampaged through the city, shooting foreigners on sight, and burning and looting homes. From other cities, white refugees fled to Shanghai and troops representing the foreign powers in the International Settlement braced to meet the "Red hordes" marching toward Shanghai's gates. War seemed inevitable. Communist troops rose in the Chinese section of Shanghai and took control from the local war lord, and Mao Tse-tung, who had assumed leadership of the party, announced that "several hundred million peasants will rise like a tornado and . . . rush forward along the road to revolution."

The war between yellow and white was not to be. Instead, there came a break between Chiang's Nationalists and Mao's Communists that has lasted to the present day.

Chiang, whose rise to the top was carefully planned, had secretly negotiated with bankers in Shanghai for financial aid and other considerations, offering in return the attractions of a non-Communist regime and the avoidance of war. Once a bargain was struck, Chiang's coup turned the revolution from left to right. A massacre of all the Communists that could be rounded up took place in Shanghai, Nanking, and Canton.

Once in power, Chiang established his new Nationalist government in Nanking and, through a series of tortuous negotiations, prevailed upon other anti-Communist factions in Peking to join forces with him. Communists were outlawed, Russian advisors expelled, and in little more than a year the unification of all China came close to reality.

Chiang's one remaining enemy was the Communists, who refused to vanish from the scene. From the beginning, Mao Tse-tung had disagreed with Moscow, which expected and planned for revolt by the urban masses. Mao based his movement on the peasants—on improving their historically miserable lot, not least by insisting that commanders pay for any village goods or services supplied to their troops. Such fairness and consideration was unprecedented, and good will toward the Communist armies steadily grew throughout rural China.

In one year alone, Chiang Kai-shek launched five separate campaigns of "bandit extermination" against the Communists, each of which ended in failure. Finally, in 1934, he succeeded in encircling them and cutting off their supply of salt and other basic commodities. After a year of blockade, the Communists—100,000 men and perhaps 50,000 women and children—broke through the Nationalist ring and began their historic Long March to remote Shensi province. Only one in five survived the six thousand-mile trek, but the behavior and discipline of the Communists along the route won them the admiration and allegiance of millions of peasants. Within a year new recruits more than made up the losses experienced on the Long March.

While Chiang Kai-shek was chasing Communists, Japan had gobbled up all of Manchuria and established the puppet empire of Manchukuo. In 1932 the Japanese moved out of their base in the International Settlement and attacked Shanghai. A long and bloody battle followed, a struggle in which Chiang showed little interest. Instead, he raised new forces in 1936 for yet another anti-Red campaign, but his troops, who wanted to fight the invaders, grumbled openly. When Chiang visited his men in the field he was arrested and threatened with execution unless he agreed to fight Japanese instead of Communists. An agreement, skillfully negotiated by Chou En-lai, was reached whereby the civil war was ended. Chiang was to remain head of state and of the army, but the legality of the Communist Party was recognized. On the surface it looked as though Chiang had won a victory. Actually, it was the Communists, hailed for their patriotism, who gained an advantage.

Beginning in 1937, when the Japanese attacked and captured Peking, the war escalated and became part of the world conflict that began with Hitler's conquest of Poland and reached its peak after Pearl Harbor. Viewed in retrospect, the behavior of the participants in the eight-year period that ended after Hiroshima resembled that of ritual dancers in a bloody and macabre drama. While Reds and Nationalists alike opposed the Japanese enemy, it was all too clear that hatred between the two was deep as ever.

The Communists fought one kind of war, the Nationalists another. Mao Tse-tung's forces operated mostly in the north, taking orders from headquarters in Yenan. Theirs were guerrilla actions, the sort that were to become all too familiar to American soldiers who fought the Vietcong in later years. As city after city fell to the Japanese, along with outward control of the roads, villages, and railways, the Communists struck quickly and then disappeared into the countryside. Japan answered with savage reprisals, burning villages and destroying rice crops. Peasant resistance to the invaders only hardened, and puppet troops enlisted by the Japanese frequently deserted and sold or turned their weapons over to the Communists.

The Nationalists fought a different kind of war. For a time they held off the Japanese at Shanghai and slowed their advance by blasting the Yellow River dikes and diverting its course—a desperate expedient that drowned innumerable noncombatants. But in time Shanghai and the other great cities near the coast fell to the invaders, with attending massacres of the inhabitants. Chiang's Nationalist government retreated to Chungking into rugged country beyond the Yangtze River gorges, where it did little or no fighting except to defend the mountain passes leading to its hideaway.

For a time they had a good excuse. When Burma fell to the onrushing Japanese the last supply road into China was cut. Within a year, however, American planes began to fly arms, ammunition, and food over the Himalayan "Hump" —first a trickle, then a steady stream, and finally, with General Joseph Stilwell's reopening of the Burma Road, a torrent. Through it all, Chiang refused to take the offensive. His responses to American pleas were threats to surrender to the Japanese, or demands for more of everything. The few keen observers on the scene, like Stilwell, who realized that Chiang was preparing for his next bout with the Communists and that Chungking was the corrupt center of a vast black-market operation, were ignored or removed from their posts. When men like Owen Lattimore and John Stewart Service pointed out that the Communists were better fed, better organized, and fighting the war with far greater effect than their Nationalist counterparts, they were branded then, and for years afterward, as "Commies."

After the surrender of Japan, General George C. Marshall came to China as American ambassador and tried for months to work out a compromise. But Chiang wanted no part of a coalition government and the Communists' attitude, at best, was equivocal. Marshall's task was hopeless and by mid-1946 civil war raged.

By this time Mao Tse-tung had established firm control over many of the northern provinces and perhaps forty percent of the population. Chiang's armies, however, were far larger and he had at his command a vast arsenal of American-supplied weapons. The Communists for the most part used guns they had captured from the Japanese.

Nonetheless, Chiang's cause proved hopeless. The morale of his men was low and sank lower. If paid at all, it was in money made worthless by the runaway inflation that swept Nationalist-held territory; at the same time, Chiang's generals were doing a brisk black-market business in American dollars. Unlike the Communists, who had involved in local government the peasants of each area they occupied, Chiang Kai-shek had made no reforms, and his peasant troops were well aware of it. His soldiers also became acutely aware of the fact that Mao's army was far better fed, better treated, and better led. Gradually at first, and then more rapidly, an attrition of Chiang's forces took place as his men deserted or changed sides. The beginning of the end came when Chiang's best troops surrendered after a badly planned and misguided drive into remote Manchuria. Nanking and Shanghai were taken and after that all of South China. On October 1, 1949, the People's Republic was proclaimed in Peking. Chiang Kai-shek and his remaining followers took refuge on the island of Taiwan and set up a republic of their own—a government that most of the "free world," led by the United States, tenaciously supported for more than twenty years.

During that period, the People's Republic emerged as a third great nuclear power on the world scene. For years, while Russia and China backed Communist or insurgent uprisings in Africa and Latin America and poured arms and supplies into Korea and Vietnam, western leaders were haunted by the specter of the two colossi striding arm in arm together toward world domination.

Only in recent years has the realization dawned on capitalist nations that perhaps unbridgeable differences exist between the two vast Communist countries, stemming from nationalistic aspirations rather than ideological goals.

Today, as western eyes are permitted glimpses of the new China that has been built in the last two decades, there is no doubt that Chairman Mao and Chou En-lai have many additional problems to solve. But there is no doubt of the growing industrial might of China, stoked by the hands and brains of seven hundred million increasingly literate human beings, nor that the world's future, in large measure, depends on how well or how badly the western world will get along with the awe-inspiring Chinese giant.

After Sun Yat-sen's death, China fell
into turmoil as Nationalists, Communists,
and war lords struggled for power.
Scenes on these pages date from those
times: A cavalry unit on shaggy Mongolian
horses in 1926, and weaponless troops
retreating from Peking in 1928.

Dissension in China enabled Japan to pursue her interests in Manchuria, where she had won a foothold during war with Russia early in century. Opposite: Japanese army (top) and marines establish puppet state of Manchukuo in 1932. Japan's attacks on China itself began the same year with assault on Shanghai which Chinese (below) were ill-equipped to defend.

In late thirties, Japanese troops
overran much of China, but could not
swallow it all. Despite brutal success
of seasoned soldiers like these,
both Chiang and the Communists
survived to fight another day.

UNITED PRESS INTERNATIONAL ▲

SOVFOTO ▲

Resolution of revolutionary struggle
came at end of World War II, when Communist
forces (left and below) swept
demoralized, ill-led, ill-fed Nationalists
(right) out of China and
established present Red regime.

WORLD WAR

II 1939-1945

When the guns fell silent in 1918—temporarily, as it developed—a dazed and shell-shocked globe clung briefly to the hope that a brave new world would be created, a world of justice and tranquility, free of secret diplomacy and under-the-table transactions between nations. The dream faded at Versailles when the victorious Allies met to design the postwar structure that was to supplant the dead-and-gone dynasties—Hohenzollern, Hapsburg, Romanov. The peace that emerged bit by bit from the conference tables was a patchwork reflecting the fears, the hatreds, and the greed of the winning side.

Woodrow Wilson compromised some of his cherished goals in order to create the League of Nations. In his own country, however, disillusionment with his ideas was fast setting in, and with it an escalating distaste for foreign entanglements. Broken in health, Wilson stood by helplessly as the Congress rejected United States entrance into the League.

In refusing to assume political leadership in a world which had seen the British empire dominant for a century, the United States eagerly sought preeminence in other fields. American dollars financed a period of shaky prosperity in Europe and South America, while her new way of life, variously described as the Era of Wonderful Nonsense and the Jazz Age, had its impact in every corner of the globe.

The twenties were an era when two things mattered: having fun and making money. It was a time of political scandal, prohibition, and organized crime; of flappers and fast cars; corsetless mothers and bathtub gin; hero worship of such disparate types as Charles Lindbergh and English Channel swimmers; and a time of relaxed morals and tense nerves which sought relief on couches presided over by disciples of Sigmund Freud.

Postwar Germany was late to discover the Philosophy of Having a Good Time. There were daily battles in the streets as splinter Communist groups fought with gangs of ex-army freebooters—*Freikorps* they were called—in abortive attempts to replace the infant republic with governments of the left or right. Then, when a semblance of order was restored, the nation went through ruinous inflation, a period when billions of marks bought a few pounds of potatoes.

By the mid-twenties, however, it seemed that Germany had weathered the storm. An attempted coup in Bavaria had been crushed and its leader was in Landsberg Prison writing an interminable book eventually to be christened *Mein Kampf*. The economy, supported largely by American loans, was beginning to boom, and unemployment was sharply down.

The picture was deceptive, however, for a great many Germans believed they hadn't lost the war but had, somehow, been cheated out of victory, betrayed at Versailles, and deprived of their long-dreamed-of "Place in the Sun" by bloated capitalists and scheming radicals, two words, which Adolf Hitler had already translated into "Jews."

The myth of German prosperity collapsed abruptly when the Wall Street crash of 1929 sent shock waves of economic depression around the world. The unemployment figures in Germany soared to unprecedented levels, and Hitler's army of Storm Troopers enrolled laid-off clerks and factory workers by tens of thousands. The chance to wear a uniform and carry a stick, whip, or club, and maybe someday a real gun with bullets, was infinitely superior to standing in a bread line.

When Hitler was appointed Chancellor of Germany in 1933, his Nazi party had never gained a majority in any election. The largest and best organized political party, it had lost ground in the last balloting, but rightist leaders of other parties, mistakenly believing they could handle Hitler, maneuvered him into office. Within a few months the Nazis seized absolute power.

The story of the next six years is too familiar to bear repeating. The democratic nations, most of whom vaguely sympathized with the German cries of unfair treatment at Versailles, stood by while Hitler crushed civil liberties, persecuted Jews and liberal leaders, quit the League of Nations, tore up the treaties restricting rearmament, sent troops to reoccupy the Rhineland, and took over Austria.

The League of Nations had become a mockery and the positions of France and England were weak. On paper they appeared strong: England was tied to France, and France's position rested on a series of mutual defense pacts with Russia and Czechoslovakia. But the appearances were illusory. France, bled white in the Great War, was appalled by any thought of a second war and was willing to take almost any measures to avoid it. England felt much the same. Thus it was, when Hitler thundered that Germany would go to war against Czechoslovakia to bring Sudeten Germans into their homeland, millions of Britishers agreed with Prime Minister Neville Chamberlain's view of the situation: "How horrible, fantastic, incredible it is that we should be digging trenches . . . because of a quarrel in a faraway country between people of whom we know nothing."

During a meeting in Munich, from which Russia was excluded, the faraway country was sold down the river to Hitler, and the Sudetenland, which contained most of the formidable Czech defensive system, reverted to Germany. Hitler promised to respect the integrity of the rump Czech state, but less than six months later marched his troops into Prague and swallowed up the remnants of the country.

At long last, with their network of alliances a shambles, England and France awoke to their peril. They hastily guaranteed to protect Poland in case of attack and set out to see what could be done to patch up the mutual defense arrangements with the Russians. Stalin, always distrustful of the democracies and miffed at Russia's exclusion from Munich, would have no part of it. In August, 1939, a dazed world learned that Germany and Russia, assumed to be the deadliest of enemies, had signed a nonaggression treaty. Just seven days later, the rebuilt German war machine swept across Polish borders, and the hour which England and France had so long dreaded struck.

While the French and English looked on helplessly, Poland was crushed in less than three weeks, and Russian troops, making good on a secret provision of the treaty with Germany, marched in and joined in a partition of the country. For six months thereafter, Allied troops waited for an attack that never came. Finally, in April of 1940, Nazi forces occupied Denmark and Norway, smashing the valiant but hopeless resistance of Norwegians and British troops who had been landed to help them.

A month later, as Winston Churchill took over Britain's government from Chamberlain, the German juggernaut again rumbled into action. In an expanded version of the Schlieffen plan, a massive right wing swept through Holland, Belgium, and Luxembourg. As a devastating rain of bombs fell on Rotterdam and other cities, paratroopers floated down to surprise and overwhelm the defenses of Liége. Simultaneously, an armored wedge of tanks and troop carriers ploughed through the heavily wooded Ardennes, created a huge gap in the French line, and raced northward to the English Channel, cutting off and encircling the retreating armies in Belgium. The Belgians surrendered and 400,000 British and French troops, huddled in and around Dunkirk, on the channel coast, were left to their fate.

The 1940 equivalent of the 1914 Miracle of the Marne followed. Confident that the *Luftwaffe* could wipe out the British and French forces caught in the steel trap, and believing he would need his armor to complete the destruction of the remaining French armies, Hitler took his tanks out of action. In the next week, an armada of destroyers and small craft lifted more than 340,000 British and French soldiers from the beaches and returned them to England. Although they had lost arms and ammunition and posed no threat to Germany at the time, their escape proved to be a strong morale builder and supplied a nucleus around which future armies were built.

France, which had believed in 1941 that it could avoid bloodletting by burying its men in the supposedly impregnable Maginot Line fortifications, lasted only a few weeks. In June the German armies paraded through the streets of Paris. Defeated and defeatist, France under Marshal Henri Philippe Pétain, the superannuated hero of Verdun, surrendered in the same railway car at Compiègne, outside Paris, in which the Germans had signed the armistice in 1918.

England, inspired by Churchill's leadership, fought on alone and prepared to resist invasion. For a few weeks, Hitler waited impatiently for an offer of surrender. When it didn't come he sent his *Luftwaffe* aloft to stamp out British resistance. During the Battle of Britain that followed, Spitfires and Hurricanes, aided by a sophisticated radar network that baffled the Nazis, proved more than a match for German fighters and bombers. After hundreds of his planes had gone down in flames, Hitler abandoned all invasion plans and contented himself with the bombing of Britain.

Reluctantly concluding that British surrender was not imminent, Hitler set plans in motion for Barbarossa, a lightning campaign to crush Russia. Once the Soviet regime had toppled, the last British hope of survival would be dead.

True, it meant a war on two fronts, which every German military man dreaded, but England was no real threat. As for Russia: Kick the door in and the whole rotten structure will come crumbling down, Hitler declared.

As the months of preparation for the Russian invasion passed, Italy proved a liability. An attack on Greece collapsed and in the Libyan desert a tiny British force annihilated an Italian army. Hitler was forced to divert troops and planes preparing for the Russian advance to crush a revolt in Yugoslavia and to blast the Greek armies and British troops landed to help them.

In June, 1941, the most awesome surprise attack in history began when three huge armored thrusts roared across the Russian border toward Leningrad in the north, Moscow in the center, and Kiev in the south. The Russian defenses went down like tenpins. By mid-July, the Nazi spearhead had pushed four hundred and fifty miles to Smolensk, along the same road Napoleon had followed in 1812 to Moscow, and the *Wehrmacht* neared Leningrad. The Russian cause seemed hopeless.

During the waning summer weeks Hitler diverted his tanks to round up and destroy the Russian armies in the south. Although more than 650,000 prisoners were taken, precious time was lost and it wasn't until October that the drive on Moscow was resumed. By that time the Russians had new allies—mud first, then ice, snow, and temperatures far below zero. The German advance slowed and, almost within sight of the Kremlin, ground to a halt. On December 6, as planes were leaving the decks of Japanese carriers to attack Pearl Harbor, the Russian counteroffensive, led by fresh divisions rushed from Siberia, began. As the shivering German troops retreated in their first major setback, a new wave of totalitarian conquest began in the Pacific.

While American sympathies had largely been with the British and French from the beginning, it was not until France fell that the United States embarked on a policy just short of war. Franklin Roosevelt's warning that the United States could not become "a lone island in a world dominated by the philosophy of force" was followed by the exchange with Great Britain of fifty World War I destroyers for seven Atlantic naval bases. Within a year of the French collapse, a massive rearmament program was under way, the nation's first peacetime draft called up 800,000 youths, American ships began to convoy supplies to England, and a lend-lease program, eventually to cost upward of $50 billion, was approved by Congress.

Meanwhile, war with Japan came closer. In July, 1941, Japan took Indochina from the puppet French regime and a freeze on petroleum imports from America left the prowar faction in Tokyo with a now-or-never feeling. The Japanese High Command had planned the Pearl Harbor attack in 1940. With a bellicose new premier, General Hideki Tojo, at the helm, the attack was approved in early September, 1941. Yet, when the bombing came, the United States, which had broken the Japanese code and knew that war was coming, was caught napping. As Japanese planes returned to their carriers, the United States Navy appeared crippled beyond repair and the road to Japanese conquest was open. A few days later, Germany and Italy declared war on the last of the big democracies.

German and Japanese fortunes in 1942 reached floodtide on every front. In the Pacific, disaster followed disaster for the Allies. Wake Island, Singapore, the Philippines, the Solomons, Sumatra, Java, Timor, most of Burma, and half of New Guinea—the string of defeats seemed endless.

On the high seas German submarines, hunting in wolf packs, took a staggering toll in the Atlantic, sending freighters to the bottom within sight of the American mainland. In North Africa British forces were sent reeling back to the gates of Alexandria. In Russia the German armies reached Stalingrad and the oil wells of the Caucasus.

A startling reversal of fortune began in midyear in the Pacific when American planes spotted a vast Japanese armada at Saipan. In the ensuing Battle of Midway, carrier and ground-based planes reduced four Japanese carriers to blazing hulks. Exactly eight months after the tragedy at Pearl Harbor, American marines stormed ashore at Guadalcanal, the first step on the long road to Tokyo.

The swing of the pendulum in the Battle of the Atlantic came during the autumn months of 1942. Long-range planes from Newfoundland, and later the Caribbean, spotted U-boats a thousand or more miles at sea. By spring, nearly one German submarine was going to the bottom for every Allied ship sunk.

The German offensive in Egypt, which had ground to a halt even as Mussolini was preparing for a triumphant entry into Alexandria, never got started again. In October, British forces led by new generals, Sir Harold Alexander and Bernard L. Montgomery, overwhelmed the German position at El Alamein. Within a few weeks, several thousand Italian and German survivors fled 700 miles westward to the Tunisian border. At the same time the first major landing operation of American and British troops stormed ashore in Morocco and western Tunisia. In an effort to keep a toehold in Africa, Hitler poured more troops and tanks into Tunisia and occupied Vichy France.

The war reached its bloodiest peak on the Volga, where since September General Friedrich von Paulus's Sixth Army had fought yard by yard for possession of Stalingrad. By mid-November the Russian defenses were reduced to rubble and the Germans had reached a state of exhaustion. North and south of the city poorly equipped Hungarian, Rumanian, and Italian troops held the Axis lines. In November, six Russian armies tore gaping holes in their defenses and trapped the entire Nazi army within the city. Hitler again ordered his troops to stand fast, but after relief forces sent to lift the siege were turned back a German retreat began. The divisions left in Stalingrad surrendered to the Russians early in 1943, and 91,000 men—all that remained of a crack army of more than 300,000—were marched off to captivity. Only 5,000 ever returned to Germany.

The two years that followed Stalingrad witnessed an ascending string of Axis setbacks. General Douglas MacArthur and Admiral Chester Nimitz perfected a technique of island-hopping that left Japanese garrisons stranded and helpless in the Pacific.

The roll call of American landings was a long one: Guadalcanal, Tarawa, Kwajalein, Saipan, Tinian, Peleliu —names that became synonymous with heavy American losses and catastrophic ones for the Japanese. The Japanese fought with fanatical bravery and when many of the islands finally fell, the few survivors committed suicide. By autumn of 1944, a vast new armada of American ships spearheaded by scores of aircraft carriers controlled the Pacific and MacArthur waded ashore in the Philippines to fulfill the promise he had made nearly three years before: "I shall return."

Hitler lost all of North Africa in the spring of 1943 with the fall of Tunis and Bizerte. The attempt to fight it out in Tunisia cost the Axis 350,000 men, a toll as great as Stalingrad. Soon after, Sicily was taken and the first Allied troops landed on the European mainland near the tip of the Italian boot. With startling suddenness, the once-awesome Fascist state collapsed when Mussolini was booted out of office and arrested. He was later snatched from under the nose of his guards by Nazi paratroopers and placed by Hitler in charge of a puppet Fascist government in northern Italy. Mussolini was by then, however, a senile and deflated man concerned only with his failing digestive tract and nagging mistress. German troops took over the fight in Italy.

With Dwight D. Eisenhower in command, American and British troops landed on Normandy beaches on D-Day, June 6, 1944. Only in one area, Omaha Beach, were casualties as great as had been expected. The build-up continued for two months and then, in the first week of August, General George Patton began his famous end run, a lightning sweep south and then east of Normandy which threatened to trap the Nazi armies near the English Channel and which paused only momentarily when Patton sent Eisenhower the message from east of Paris, "Dear Ike—Today I have spat in the Seine." Paris was liberated amid wild rejoicing as Free French forces rolled through the city's streets. With half a million men dead and virtually all of their equipment lost, the remaining German troops in France streamed back toward the Rhine. By October, the first German city, Aachen, was taken.

Hitler's secret weapons, the V-1 buzz bomb and the more dangerous V-2 rocket, forerunner of the missiles that were to take men to the moon, were launched in 1944, but their threat was wiped out when launching sites were overrun by advancing American and British armies. With the skies over Germany completely in their control, American bombings by day and British by night blasted German cities to rubble. While the toll in lives and property was horrendous, the air attacks broke neither the German spirit nor, until the very end, reduced the country's industrial output.

For a time the Nazis held near the prewar borders. A British attempt to invade Germany through Holland collapsed with severe losses and Hitler was able to mount one limited offensive, his last, in December, 1944, against American troops in the Ardennes. It got only as far as the Meuse River.

The last German offensive in Russia, Operation Citadel, began on a narrow front in the late spring of 1943 and ended in two weeks when a huge concentration of Nazi tanks took what proved to be a death ride against Russian defenses. From then on the initiative passed irrevocably to the Red armies. Beginning at Kharkov, the Nazi armies retraced their steps through lands they had overrun in 1941, sometimes in a step-by-step retreat, sometimes in panicky flight, leaving behind them scorched ruins, mass graves of their victims, and hundreds of thousands of their own dead. By the end of 1944, Hitler's allies had surrendered or changed sides and Russian troops were fighting in East Prussia.

The final German collapse came in 1945. Early in the year, an overwhelming tide of Russian men and machines rolled over the German defenses. Vienna fell in April, and by the end of the month Red troops were fighting in the suburbs of Berlin. In the West, American forces seized a partially destroyed bridge crossing the Rhine at Remagen, opening a road that led to the heart of Germany. Other Rhine crossings came soon afterward and British and Canadian troops encircled a huge mass of Germans in the industrial Ruhr Valley.

As American armies raced toward a juncture with Russian troops on the Elbe, they came upon several of the monstrous slaughterhouses Hitler had built at Buchenwald, Auschwitz, Dachau, Belsen, and dozens of other locations. In these camps millions of Jews, along with dissenters and liberals, had gone to their death in various ways, all diabolical. Some were asphyxiated by gas in specially constructed shower-baths, some were gunned to death in craters they themselves had dug, and some died as human guinea pigs in scientific experiments. As part of Hitler's "final solution" to the Jewish problem, bodies were consumed in giant crematoria, but such adjuncts as shoes, hair, and gold fillings were carefully preserved and re-used.

Momentarily cheered by news of Franklin Roosevelt's death, Hitler kept hoping for a last-minute miracle. When one didn't come and when Russian troops had fought their way within a few hundred yards of his underground bunker, the Nazi leader played out the last scene of his *Götterdämmerung*. He married Eva Braun, who had been his mistress for more than twelve years, and saw to it that his dog Blondi was poisoned. The next day Eva took poison and Hitler shot himself through the mouth. Their gasoline-soaked bodies were burned in the chancellery garden.

Japan fought on alone following the German surrender. Two of her strongest defensive island outposts, Iwo Jima and Okinawa, went early in 1945 after an inch-by-inch defense. From flying fields that ringed the Japanese islands, B-29 bombers pulverized city after city. A single raid on Tokyo killed nearly 100,000, wounded 125,000, and left more than a million homeless. In last-ditch attempts to stave off the inevitable, hundreds of Kamikaze pilots used their planes as weapons in suicide dives on American warships, while Japan's last and largest battleship was sent into battle with only enough fuel for a one-way trip.

The United States invasion of Japan that had been carefully planned was never launched, for the first atomic bomb was dropped on the city of Hiroshima. "I regarded [it] as a military weapon and never had any doubt it should be used," President Harry S. Truman wrote in retrospect. Two days later, Russia declared war on Japan and invaded Manchuria, and the following day a plutonium bomb destroyed Nagasaki. The Japanese quickly surrendered and in mid-August six years of killing came to an end.

Any attempt to assess the costs of the vast conflict is futile. Most authorities estimate battle deaths at 30,000,000 with Russia accounting for one-quarter of the total. In addition to the extermination of more than half of Europe's 10,000,000 Jews, millions of others met death from the air, starved to death during the three-year siege of Leningrad, or died from malnutrition or overwork as slave laborers in German industrial plants.

The ultimate effect of the vast conflict is equally uncertain. The Fascist states vanished, but a confrontation between democratic societies and totalitarian Communist regimes began in 1945 and has lasted to the present day.

Just one fact is certain: With the creation of atomic weapons mankind acquired, at long last, the capacity to destroy completely all life on earth.

German *Wehrmacht*, secretly rebuilt
despite restrictions of Versailles Treaty,
emerged in public soon after Hitler came to power
in 1933. Here, a year later, the *Feldjäger*
Korps parades before *der Führer* at
Nuremberg rally. Following pages: Overview
of massed Nazis at Nuremberg.

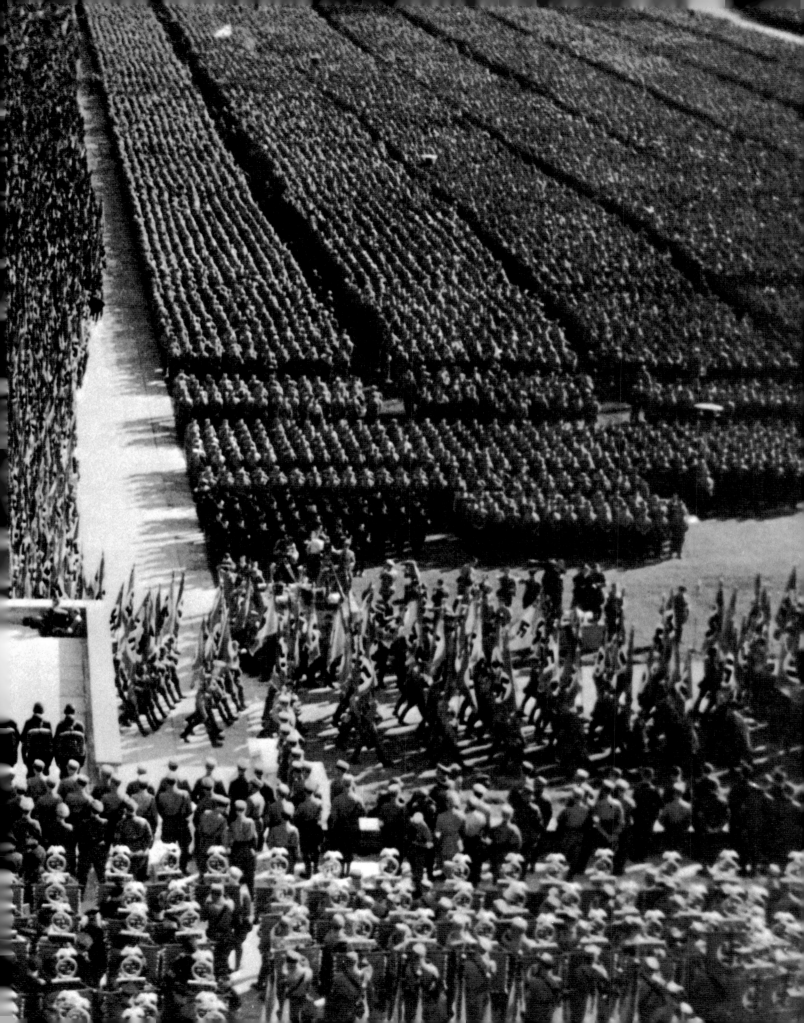

After France fell, England fought on
alone. Hitler sent bombers across the Channel
by the hundreds in a prelude to what was
to have been an amphibious landing
on British shores. German photograph above
shows two Dornier 217s flying over
fires they started near a London gas works.
Opposite: London street after biggest
German night raid of the war. Following
pages: Ruins of bombed London, and
patient Britons in air-raid shelter
during winter of 1940-41.

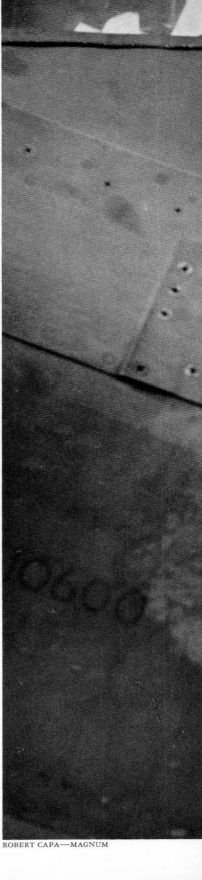

Top: German pilots at lunch, with
Messerschmitt 109s in background, somewhere
on eastern front, probably during destruction
of Poland. Above: American B-17s flew
bombing missions from Europe to the Pacific.
Opposite: England, 1941. Spitfire pilot,
with one Italian and nine German
planes to his credit, lands after mission.
Following pages: When tide turned, Allied
bombers rained devastation on
Germany. This is Cologne, late in war.

War in the Desert, 1942: British infantrymen rush German tank knocked out during one of many battles for North Africa. Following pages: Horde of Russian prisoners captured by Germans on eastern front. Most of these men probably became slave laborers.

Opposite: Action during crucial Battle of
Stalingrad. Eventually, Germans and
Russians fought for inches amid rubble.
Below: Russian farm boys being carted to front.
Bottom: German prisoners at Stalingrad.

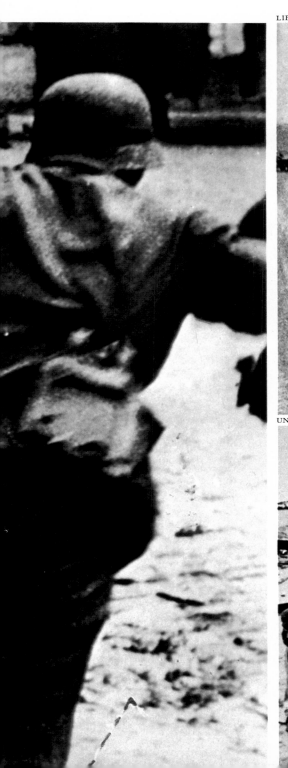

LIFE

UNITED PRESS INTERNATIONAL ▼

In Pacific, U.S. forces inexorably
destroyed Japanese navy and exterminated ground
troops in island strongholds. Below: Elements
of U.S. fleet, with carrier *Essex* in foreground.
Opposite: Assault on Eniwetok, 1944.

Japanese dead on beach near Buna Mission, New Guinea, 1943.

Nicosia (opposite) and Troina—
two tough and not very memorable
fights in effort to drive Axis out of
Sicily and then Italy in 1943.

ROBERT CAPA—MAGNUM

Omaha Beach at close of D-Day. Normandy fishermen view dead about to be evacuated.

Battle of the Bulge was Germany's
last offensive effort, an armored thrust
to halt the Allies surging toward
the homeland. Nazis above are fighting
units of American 1st Army. Opposite are
British reinforcements advancing to
front to Ardennes forest, and
American tanks going to relief of
troops surrounded in Bastogne.

Aftermath: French woman accused of
collaboration with Germans is harried through
streets of Chartres by jeering townspeople
after liberation of area by Allies.

ROBERT CAPA—MAGNUM

Above: American 17th Airborne Division parachutes
into Germany after Rhine was crossed. Opposite:
One of the last casualties in Europe:
an American killed in Leipzig the day war ended.

Belsen, 1945. One of 60,000
starving, sick, and dying
inmates of Nazi horror camp.
Many died even as British
army tried to save them.
This man, too weak to walk,
had been without water
for six days. Following
pages: Aerial view of
part of Hiroshima after
A-bomb dropped, killing
—instantly or eventually—
some 100,000 Japanese.

KOREAN WA

R 1950-1953

In June, 1950, the world awoke to find itself again at war. Some 80,000 North Korean troops, following waves of Russian-built tanks, had crossed the invisible line dividing the peninsula and begun an unexpected invasion of South Korea.

During World War II, Roosevelt, Churchill, and Stalin had agreed that a free Korea was desirable but that the country might require a period of apprenticeship. Forty years, Stalin indicated, would be about right. The division of the country at the 38th Parallel was an afterthought and came about with the quick capitulation of Japan after atomic bombs were dropped on Hiroshima and Nagasaki. "We expected that the division of the country would be solely for the purpose of accepting the Japanese surrender," Harry S. Truman said later, "and that joint control would then extend throughout the peninsula."

It didn't work out that way. Three years after the war ended, North Korea had been massively communized, and Stalin, no longer referred to as Uncle Joe, looked blank whenever the question of Korean unification was raised. As early as 1946, elections for "People's Committees" were held in North Korea. More than ninety-three percent of the voting population marched to the polls past campaign posters reading: "For the Fatherland, for the Party, for Stalin." It was a great example of "loyalty" to the new regime, Truman said, but then "the voters did not have the embarrassment of having to choose between candidates. There was only one slate."

The South held its own elections in 1948. They resulted in the creation of the Republic of Korea with a little-known rightist named Syngman Rhee as its first President, a gentleman who from the outset of his regime displayed a startling lack of managerial talent. The Russians countered the move a month later by announcing the formation of the Democratic People's Republic of Korea.

The Sunday morning attack, reminiscent of Pearl Harbor, came as a surprise to world capitals, notably Washington. Throughout the spring, intelligence reports had told of the build-up of North Korean troops, of increased guerrilla activities south of the border, and of the possibility of a major attack. But the reports were discounted since they listed many other trouble spots throughout the world, as well.

There was another reason for American de- tachment. Since the war's end, American eyes had been trained in other directions: Europe, where in Berlin and the Balkans things got messier day by day; and China, where Chiang Kai-shek's regime had reached the end of the line at its offshore stronghold of Taiwan. As a result, efforts to train and equip the South Korean army had been haphazard.

When news came of the invasion, Truman moved fast. A meeting of the United Nations Security Council unanimously (no Russian representative was present) ordered the North Koreans to stop their attack and withdraw. At the same time orders went to the top American commander in Japan, General Douglas MacArthur, telling him to rush supplies to the South Koreans.

The Korean People's Army, which had learned quickly from its Russian instructors, moved even faster. It captured Seoul, the South Korean capital, within four days and went on to overrun virtually the whole peninsula. MacArthur took a quick look at the situation and reported that "South Korean casualties as an index to fighting have not shown adequate resistance possibilities or the will to fight and our estimate is that a complete collapse is imminent."

Two days after the invasion began, the United Nations made Korea its first "police action," and a few days later the first Americans, comprising the 24th Infantry Division, landed with instructions to slow down the enemy advance. MacArthur was given over-all command of what eventually proved to be troops from eleven nations.

Vain, imperious, and stubborn, MacArthur also happened to be a highly talented military leader who had made an enormous contribution to the 1942-1945 victory in the Pacific. Dubbed the "Viceroy of Japan" as a result of his role in the postwar military occupation of that nation, he came up with a plan to retake Korea that met with disfavor on all sides. Nonetheless, it worked.

The First Marine Division spearheaded an amphibious landing at Inchon, the port of Seoul. The difficulties inherent in taking the port, with its erratic tides, limited pier space, and steep beachwalls, MacArthur pointed out, "will ensure for me the element of surprise . . . for the enemy commander will reason that no one would be so brash as to make such an attempt."

Preceding pages: U.S. Marines retreat
from Changjin Reservoir area of North Korea.

As the invading marines landed, the South Korean forces who had managed to cling to a tiny perimeter of land at Pusan also took the offensive, and in short order the battle groups met and converged on Seoul. The General and President Rhee entered the shattered capital, and in the euphoria of the moment a new and glittering concept began to take shape—a vision of an all-out victory and the reunification of Korea, in place of the lackluster policy of containment and maintenance of the status quo.

MacArthur had presidential authority to go north of the border if, and only if, there was no threat of intervention from either Russian or Chinese forces. This seeming to be the case, troops crossed the 38th Parallel, and shortly thereafter the United Nations tacitly approved the move. As the victorious Eighth Army approached Pyongyang, the capital of North Korea, MacArthur and Truman met for the first and only time on Wake Island. "The general assured me that the victory was won in Korea," Truman said. "He also informed me that the Chinese Communists would not attack."

But as the United Nations forces approached the Yalu River, which marked the border between North Korea and Manchuria, it began to dawn on the victorious Allies that quite a few of their prisoners were Chinese regulars. At first MacArthur discounted the extent of Chinese involvement, but on November 6, the day before the American election, Truman was shocked to learn that bombing of the Yalu bridges, on a large scale, had been ordered. Asked for an explanation, the General said that "men and material in large force are pouring over all bridges" and "threaten the ultimate destruction of the forces under my command."

It soon was apparent that MacArthur had been monumentally wrong in predicting that China could not and would not intervene on a large scale. More than 300,000 Chinese troops had crossed the border and it seemed to Truman and his advisors that Chairman Mao was indeed willing to risk a major war. MacArthur, however, had recovered from his earlier fear that his troops faced destruction and begun another offensive that was intended to end the war; he went so far as to tell one of his commanders to notify the troops that they would be home by Christmas. Within four days there began, however, what became known as "the big bug-out." In the face of growing pressure, the offensive stalled and a retreat began, gradual at first, then escalating into something of a rout. By early December the retreat had carried the U.N. forces well below the Parallel.

If MacArthur was embarrassed by having made predictions that were not borne out, he didn't show it. Instead, he declared a war of his own against Truman, Secretary of State Dean Acheson, the U.N. allies who were increasingly fearful of Russian intervention, and his superiors in the American military establishment—Generals Eisenhower, Marshall, and Bradley (among others). The current defeat, he explained, was the obvious result of Truman's failure to allow him to wage unrestricted war against China.

In interviews with the press, MacArthur made no secret of his personal plan for victory. Blockade the Chinese mainland. Bomb China. Invade China with Chiang Kai-shek's troops. Use part of Chiang's forces in Korea. It was, as General Omar Bradley, speaking for the Joint Chiefs of Staff, said, "The wrong war, at the wrong place, at the wrong time and with the wrong enemy." When MacArthur was informed that another major war was not precisely what the leading nations wanted at this point, he replied that the current policy spelled the annihilation of the entire U.N. command.

MacArthur had guessed wrong again. After Matthew Ridgway became head of the Eighth Army, the tide began to turn. The Allied troops recaptured Seoul for the second time and fought their way back to the Parallel and a bit beyond. It became clear that the stalemate could only be broken by bringing Peking and North Korea to the bargaining table. MacArthur thought differently. As Senator Robert Taft and a cadre of fellow Republicans came to his defense on the home front and advocated all-or-nothing military operations, he went over Truman's head to the American public. He issued a press release stressing the lack of industrial development in China and its inability to wage a modern war, and hinting that the U.N. forces should drop their "tolerant attitude toward China" and bring about its complete military collapse. On the basis of such facts, he invited the Chinese to meet with him immediately.

Since the General had been instructed to clear all policy pronouncements through Washington, Truman was faced with a difficult decision. He made it quickly and relieved

All photographs in this section by David Douglas Duncan.

MacArthur of his command. "By this act," he said, "MacArthur left me no choice—I could no longer tolerate his insubordination." His stand was reinforced when a letter from MacArthur to House Minority Leader Joseph Martin was made public. It repeated MacArthur's belief that Asia would be the battleground of the future. It ended with the General's favorite slogan, "There is no substitute for victory."

All hell broke loose when news of MacArthur's dismissal was made public. Herbert Hoover, Senators Taft, Joseph McCarthy, and Richard Nixon all rushed in with fierce denunciations of the Administration. Each had plans, ranging from the immediate reinstatement of the General (Nixon's contribution), to impeachment proceedings (Martin's solution), and accusations of Communist conspiracy at top Government levels came from all sides. Public clamor was no less emotional, no less irrational. Truman and Acheson were burned in effigy throughout the country. MacArthur's appearance in New York City produced crowds which exceeded those that had welcomed Eisenhower after World War II. In his speech to a joint session of Congress, MacArthur dramatically concluded, "And like the old soldier of that ballad, I now close my military career, and just fade away—an old soldier who has tried to do his duty as God gave him the light to see that duty. Goodbye." He left his audience in tears.

Ridgway succeeded MacArthur and the fighting continued. In the spring of 1951 the Communists launched their biggest offensive of the war and only at a tremendous cost in human life were the U.N. forces able to hold. Ninety thousand Chinese were reportedly killed in one week.

Armistice negotiations were begun in July at Panmunjom, a village in central Korea, south of the 38th Parallel. They were to continue for two years and would be filled with erratic and often exasperating behavior on both sides. The approach to the agenda reflected real differences between the two sides. The Americans were interested in a military settlement, a cease-fire and repatriation of prisoners. The Communists emphasized the political aspects. They were primarily concerned with the establishment of the 38th Parallel as a permanent demarcation line and with the withdrawal of all foreign troops on either side. The two sides finally reached agreement on two major points: the retention of the 38th Parallel and the cease-fire. The question of repatriation of prisoners kept the war going for another fifteen months.

As the 1952 presidential campaign reached its climax, General Eisenhower made a dramatic pledge: "I shall go to Korea." In December, having won the election, he went. The brief trip confirmed his belief that an immediate settlement was imperative. Returning home, he made it clear that any delay on the part of the Communists would force an expansion of the war. A veiled threat of atomic attack lay behind his words.

Another factor contributed to a final softening on the part of the Chinese. With the death of Stalin there was a thaw in the cold-war politics of the big powers, and the Chinese Communists declared themselves ready to conclude an armistice. The Republic of Korea refused to participate. Finally, a senior negotiator from each side signed an armistice.

No formal peace treaty has ever been signed, and there remains an armed force along the 38th Parallel. What did three years of bloody fighting add up to? The Korean conflict was the first confrontation of the two dominant philosophies of modern politics. To some the conflict may have proved that the United States was willing to stand up to Communist aggression, giving meaning to the determination of the United Nations to act as a peace force in the world. Or, as Chairman Georgi Malenkov declared in a speech in Moscow, the truce could be viewed as "a victory for the peace-loving forces of the world."

In any event, both Koreas were wrecked by the war and neither has fully recovered. Military and civilian casualties were in excess of 3,000,000, almost equally divided between the sides. United Nations casualties, eighty or more percent American, were in excess of 180,000.

The goal of creating a democratic government in South Korea has never come close to realization. Rhee became progressively myopic and dictatorial and was toppled in 1960. The following year a military junta, which still maintains a tenuous rule, took over. Its leader, General Chung Hee Park, has been "elected" several times, but a true democracy, one suspects, will be a long time coming.

Marine corporal leads way past dead North
Korean during patrol action along
Naktong River perimeter. Following pages:
Korean civilians duck for safety in
Seoul railroad station as city is
recaptured after Inchon landing.

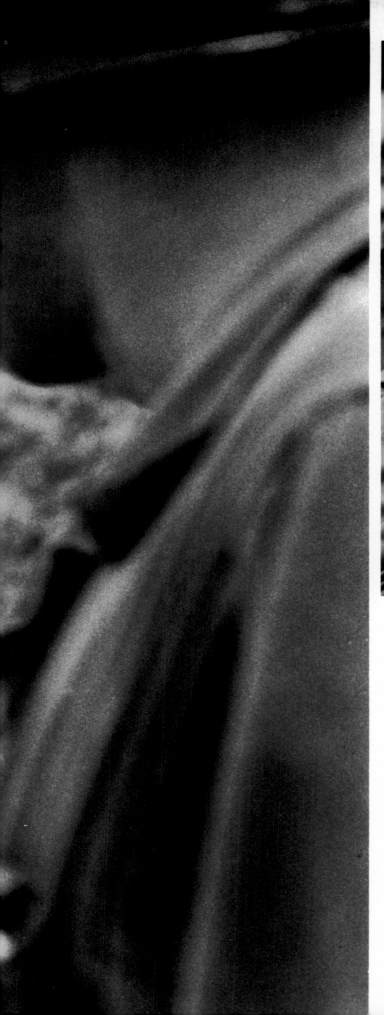

Americans in Korea, 1950. Following pages: Retreat in winter.

SIX-DAY WAR

JUNE 4-10, 1967

"We face you in battle and are burning with desire to start in order to obtain revenge. This will make the world realize what the Arabs are and what the Jews are." The voice was that of Gamal Abdel Nasser, President of the United Arab Republic. He spoke over Cairo Radio, directing his threats to the people of Israel. A few miles away the forces of the infant republic tensely faced the armor of three nations, Syria to the north, Jordan to the east, Egypt to the west and south.

The British had relinquished their mandate over Palestine in 1947, after twenty-five years of rule punctured by acts of violence and terrorism. The United Nations took over and the following year voted to partition the tiny country between Arabs and Jews. It was a decision worthy of a slightly demented Solomon, for in this case the baby was cut into three pieces, and Israel was awarded three jigsaw-puzzle bits of land. The Arabs, refusing to recognize Israel, launched a campaign of extermination but were quickly routed by the Israelis and forced to sign an armistice giving Israel half again as much territory as the U.N. had awarded it by the partition.

In 1956, after Nasser nationalized the Suez Canal, war came again. Backed by the English and French, who were angered by the Egyptian move, Israeli forces under the command of General Moshe Dayan went into action. Although Nasser had hundreds of Czech planes and tanks, it took Israel just seven days to overrun the Sinai Peninsula and reach the Canal. Subsequently, under U.N. pressure, both the Israeli and Anglo-French troops were withdrawn and Egypt agreed to permit a peacekeeping U.N. police force to be stationed in the area. The hitch was Nasser's demand, to which the United Nations agreed, that the troops be withdrawn at his request.

During the next ten years the Arab nations armed, and Russia, which had been largely instrumental in pushing the partition through the U.N. in 1948, provided a steady flow of military equipment. A United Arab Command voted in 1964 to spend $43 million a year to arm Jordan, Lebanon, and Syria.

In mid-May, 1967, Egypt formally demanded the immediate withdrawal of all U.N. troops. Secretary-General U Thant agreed meekly and mobilization in Egypt, Syria, and Israel was accelerated. In Jordan the famed Arab Legion, a modern equivalent of the force that had fought under Lawrence of Arabia, was ready for action.

A procession of new T-54 and T-34 Russian tanks clanked out of Cairo to take their positions in the Sinai Desert, and headlines announced that 80,000 "elite" troops had "marched to confront the Zionist enemy." Nasser's next move was to blockade the Gulf of Aqaba, Israel's sea lane to Asia and Africa. The Soviet Union assured Nasser of its support in enforcing the blockade, and the next day King Hussein of Jordan flew his own jet to Cairo to sign a defense pact with Nasser, his former enemy. In Israel, General Dayan once again became Defense Minister.

The odds against Israel, armed with French planes and American and British tanks, appeared overwhelming. She had around 250,000 regular and reserve troops against more than twice that many of her enemies; 800 tanks against 2,000; and 350 planes against 600.

In the early morning heat of June 5, Israel struck. Wave after wave of French-built Mystères and Mirages hit two dozen military airfields in Egypt, Syria, Iraq, and Jordan. The surprise attack caught Russian MIGs and bombers parked in neat rows. Some pilots flew eight or more missions that day. By evening close to 500 planes had been destroyed and complete control of the skies had passed to Israel. On the ground the results were even more spectacular and, from the Arab point of view, devastating. Some hours before the Israeli planes were airborne, Egyptian mortars had pumped shells across the Gaza Strip into border *kibbutzim* in what could have been the opening of hostilities or a harrassment measure—no one has ever decided. In any event, with the coming of dawn three Israeli columns of tanks and motorized infantry smashed westward across the Sinai Peninsula to encircle and cut off the escape routes of more than 100,000 Egyptians. In the north the feeble Palestinian Liberation Army, armed with Chinese rifles, was quickly trapped. By nightfall the tanks were through the minefields and racing down the coast.

The course of the war can be followed by Egyptian radio announcements. Throughout the first day they told of huge victories and a triumphal march on Tel Aviv. On the second day Nasser took to the air to tell his people—falsely—that American aircraft carriers and American and British planes had joined in the war against Egypt and Jordan.

Preceding pages: Egyptian tanks
stranded in Sinai Desert after
strikes by Israeli air and
armor destroyed Arab invasion force.

On the fifth day Nasser offered to resign and told millions of weeping Egyptians, "We cannot hide from ourselves that we have met with a grave setback in the last few days."

That was an understatement. For Egypt and Jordan it had been a four-day war. Twenty thousand Egyptians and 15,000 Jordanians were dead. The Sinai Peninsula had been overrun and Israeli soldiers were bathing in two gulfs, Suez and Aqaba.

Jordan agreed to the United Nations' demand for a cease-fire first and, eighty-five hours after the war had begun, Nasser accepted the terms as well. Syria, where the fighting had begun with an artillery duel, struggled on for another two days. By Saturday her supposedly impregnable frontier defenses (Russian-built) had collapsed and Israeli tanks were rolling toward Damascus past the wreckage of Syrian equipment and the bodies of Syrian dead. As evening of the sixth day approached, the last of the allied Arab forces called it quits, and the most one-sided war of the century came to an end. Israeli dead, most of whom lost their lives in Syria and in the battle for Jerusalem, came to 679.

"The war is over," Moshe Dayan said. "Now the trouble begins." He was, of course, right. In the sessions of the United Nations that followed the cease-fire, Israel was condemned as the aggressor and told to withdraw to her former borders, an edict she refused to obey.

The fighting had barely stopped before Russia was shipping planes and missiles and new tanks to Egypt to replace those lost in the desert. In the lands surrounding a vastly expanded Israel, guerrilla armies trained for the day when the hated enemy would meet its doom.

The Six-Day War ensured Israel's survival for some years, at least, but did nothing to ease the plight of 700,000 Arab refugees who had lived on the land for centuries before Jews returned to the place they had called home two millennia ago. Nor did it answer the even bigger question: How can a nation of two or three million survive when bordered by alien and hostile populations who outnumbered its people twenty or more to one? Perhaps the fact that Arab and Jew are the Ishmael and Isaac of the Old Testament—both Semitic, both sharing religions that are similar in many ways—will supply an eventual answer. Perhaps the great powers, notably Russia and the United States, can one day combine to enforce the restless peace that exists in the Near East.

One thing seems certain. Unless an answer can be found, there will be a fourth war and the stunning victory of 1967 will become just one more footnote in a narrative of bloodshed and enslavement that dates back to the earliest civilizations of man.

Opposite: Miles of wrecked and
burnt-out Egyptian equipment.
Top: Nasser portrait abandoned by
fleeing Arabs. Below: Israeli
soldier after victory.

Two of Egypt's Russian tanks left to die in Sinai.

Wailing Wall in Jerusalem: Jews
old and new (opposite) prepare for
prayer. Troops celebrate.

Above: Burial service at military
cemetery on Mt. Herzl in Jerusalem. Opposite:
Old woman passes ruins of Church of
Notre Dame de France in Jerusalem.

VIETNAM

1946-1973

The Vietnamese conflict was a war without beginning or end, like an interminable and confused Oriental drama in which alien characters (Japanese, French, and Americans) came upon the scene, played their roles and vanished, permitting the local actors to carry on as before.

More than eighty years of colonial rule in Vietnam ended with the collapse of France in 1940. The Japanese pounced on the country but soon discovered that their attempts to rule through French administrators were hampered by an underground opposition movement called the Viet Minh, or the League for the Independence of Vietnam. Its leader was Ho Chi Minh, a brilliant and dedicated Marxist. After Japan surrendered, the French returned and the Democratic Republic of Vietnam, with Ho Chi Minh as its leader, was recognized as a free state within the French union.

This arrangement soon fell apart and by the end of 1946 a bloody struggle between the French and the Viet Minh had begun. Ho Chi Minh warned that his people were prepared to fight for ten years, if necessary, and the French responded by recalling Bao Dai, a former emperor, and installing him as chief of state in Saigon.

After eight years of fighting, the more than 350,000 French troops in Vietnam were exhausted and bewildered. Bao Dai vanished from the scene and in 1954, following a disastrous defeat at Dien Bien Phu, France gave up her colonial claim. The mortification was not lessened by the criticism of American military observers who deplored the French habit of fighting by day and abandoning the countryside to the Viet Minh by night. If Americans were in charge, they claimed, the Reds would be wiped out in six months.

The United States didn't have to wait long for its chance to prove the point. The result was the longest and saddest war in which Americans and Vietnamese have ever fought, war in which the clenched fist and the hard hat became symbols of a divided and distraught United States.

In the summer of 1954 a temporary agreement was reached in Geneva whereby Vietnam was divided along the 17th Parallel. The land north of the line was the domain of Ho Chi Minh's followers and the southern areas went to the anti-Communists, led by a political lightweight named Ngo Dinh Diem. Elections were to be held in 1956.

Unification was not to be. As the Viet Minh took over, nearly a million North Vietnamese, mostly Catholics terrified by the Communist presence, streamed south for safety. In Saigon Diem became President of the new Republic of South Vietnam but refused to take part in any nationwide election. It was now 1955 and the second of five successive American presidents to support the Saigon regime took action. Dwight D. Eisenhower set up a Military Assistance Advisory Group (MAAG) to take over the training of the army of South Vietnam. The early advisors numbered around 300. (Truman had sent an economic mission to help the French.)

During the next five years the pace of the United States' involvement quickened. The Communists organized a National Liberation Front (NLF) and a new name appeared in American newspapers—the Vietcong. The Vietcong's resistance to Diem's policies, it was said, met with considerable success among peasants in remote regions. MAAG advisors increased to 900.

In 1961 a new President, John Fitzgerald Kennedy, faced up to some increasingly unpleasant facts. The ruling team, Diem and his brother Ngo Dinh Nhu, was acutely unpopular with most of its subjects. The threat of the Vietcong was growing fast, and the time had clearly come for the Americans to get in deeper. Or pull out.

J.F.K. didn't hesitate. "Several hundred specialists in guerrilla warfare" were sent overseas to train Vietnamese soldiers. By the end of the year "several hundred" had turned out to be more than 3,000. Casualties began to mount, but Kennedy saw "light at the end of the tunnel."

By 1963 millions of Buddhists in South Vietnam revolted against Diem's Catholic party and uprisings in Saigon and Hue were savagely stamped out. As Buddhist monks immolated themselves in protest, South Vietnam's generals solved the problem by murdering Diem and his brother. Doggedly, the American Government supported all ten governments that followed one another over the next year and a half.

In 1964 two American destroyers were reportedly attacked by North Vietnamese torpedo boats in Tonkin Gulf. President Lyndon Baines Johnson, whose bold attack on inequities in America had resulted in the most progressive social legislation in many decades, met the challenge with an enthusiastic call for action. With only two dissenting votes in the Senate and none in the House, Congress passed the Gulf of Tonkin resolution. It gave the President powers to "repel any armed attack against the forces of the United States and to prevent further aggression."

Early in 1965 a Vietcong attack on an American outpost near Pleiku was answered by the first aerial bombings north of the Parallel, and in midyear 23,000 advisors were turned overnight into combat troops and were sent into action. A new American commander, General William Westmoreland, issued the first of many calls for more men. By the close of 1965 more than 184,000 Americans took over the fighting from South Vietnamese troops, who had been displaying a distressing tendency to throw away their rifles and flee from the Vietcong.

To this point the majority of Americans had either ignored the American commitment or approved of it. After all, supporters said, South Vietnam was a brave little democracy and the country's job was to support brave little democracies and contain Communism. By the end of 1966, however, nearly 400,000 American fighting men were in Vietnam and casualties had soared to 21,000, nearly six times the preceding year's total. The increased bombings of the North hadn't slowed the movement of Russian and Chinese equipment across the so-called demilitarized zone, and embarrassing questions were being asked. Was South Vietnam really a brave little democracy? How long was the brush-fire war to go on? What were Americans doing there in the first place? Didn't they have enough problems at home?

A flood of reassuring pronouncements, from President Johnson and General Westmoreland down, failed to placate the rapidly growing ranks of dissenters in Congress and among the people. Nor were these people (called "doves," as opposed to the prowar "hawks") particularly reassured when the two generals recently elected to office, Head of State Nguyen Van Thieu and Premier Nguyen Cao Ky, tossed the runner-up (and leader of the peace party) into jail.

Television and newspaper coverage of the war expanded, and a large segment of the American public didn't like what it saw or read. It became painfully apparent that the Saigon regime closely resembled a military junta, that crime and corruption were widespread, and that the enemies encountered by American soldiers included drug addiction and venereal disease, along with fanatical Vietcong guerrillas who struck with deadly precision and than vanished into rain forests and mountains.

Loudest of the protestors were American students, most of whom had to face military service after graduation. For the first time in the nation's history a sizable number of young men elected to go to jail rather than fight in a war they disapproved of, while hundreds of others left the country to take unhappy refuge in Canada, Mexico, and Sweden. Still others, by the thousands, eluded the draft through legal loopholes or suddenly acquired medical disabilities.

Early in 1968, as American forces in Vietnam neared their peak of 535,000, the Vietcong launched its Tet (New Year's) offensive. Saigon was attacked, the United States embassy entered, and provincial towns and the countryside around them overrun. When General Westmoreland issued yet another plea for 205,000 more men, most Americans were willing to concede that the war was a mistake. What divided the country down the middle was the cry of the doves for quick and complete withdrawal, while the hawks demanded that the United States continue fighting until a successful conclusion was reached.

In March the American public saw Lyndon Johnson, his dream of a Great Society yet another victim of the Vietnam morass, announce he would not run again for the presidency and that he was limiting the bombing of North Vietnam. Talks soon began in Paris between American and North Vietnamese representatives. Westmoreland, turning over command of the army to General Creighton Abrams, confessed that an American military victory in Vietnam was not in the cards. The antiwar protests, which for the most part had been peaceful, grew larger and culminated in a pitched battle in the streets of Chicago between police and protestors outside the Democratic National Convention. In November a halt to the bombing of North Vietnam was announced and the newly elected President, Richard M. Nixon, prepared to take office.

In campaigning, Nixon had urged Americans to lower their voices and promised to reunite them by bringing the war to an end. After a year in the presidency, however, only a token withdrawal of troops had taken place and Nixon's early rise to public office on a platform of virulent anticommunism was widely pointed to as evidence of his intention to continue to escalate the war. In 1970, American troops were sent into Cambodia to clear out sanctuaries of Vietcong and North Vietnamese troops. The national roar of protest reached a climax on the campus of Kent State University in Ohio, where several students died in a hail of bullets fired by panicky and largely untrained National Guardsmen. Two months later Nixon announced that the troops had been withdrawn from Cambodia. By the close of 1970 a total of 200,000 Americans had left Vietnam, and the dead and seriously wounded, which had reached a peak of over 61,000 in 1968, dropped below 20,000.

As the months went by, most of the fighting was taken over by the South Vietnamese army, on whom billions of dollars in equipment and training had been lavished. A major invasion of Laos met disaster on the Ho Chi Minh Trail, however, as many of the newly equipped units broke and fled the battlefield with heavy casualties. The Paris talks and the protests continued.

Bombing of North Vietnam was resumed by Nixon in 1972 after another offensive, by far the biggest of the war, smashed the South Vietnam defenses in the central highlands and brought the Saigon regime to the verge of collapse. The blasting of Communist supply lines and industrial targets combined with the mining of North Vietnam harbors had their effect, however, and after some weeks the attacks sputtered and died away. In that year the last American combat battalion was pulled out of action.

A few weeks before his landslide re-election Nixon told his countrymen that talks with Hanoi conducted for nearly ten months by his special representative, Henry Kissinger, had borne fruit and that a cease-fire was soon to come. Kissinger than announced that peace was "at hand."

He was premature. Snags in the negotiations developed and both sides charged that the other had tried to change the stakes. While critics hinted that the peace statement had been issued to make certain of Nixon's re-election, Nixon ordered a resumption of the bombing of North Vietnam. This time it was on an unprecedented scale, and spearheaded by the United States air fleet of monster B-52's, which had never before been sent against heavily defended cities like Hanoi. American losses in planes were severe and hundreds of square miles of enemy territory were ravaged.

In 1973, as Congress reassembled in a sterner mood and prepared to restrict the President's warmaking powers, the end came with startling suddenness. Kissinger was once more sent to Paris and a week later Nixon and Hanoi announced simultaneously that a cease-fire would be signed in Paris. The Thieu regime in Saigon, which had fought the Washington-Hanoi rapprochement from the beginning, sullenly went along with the decision.

Fighting continues in Vietnam, but the Americans, like the French before them, have left. Hanoi claims that it won a great victory but that is by no means certain. The original involvement of the United States came about through a belief in the so-called domino theory: If the democracies did not stand up to Communist aggression and permitted one segment of the free world to topple, others would collapse in turn. Thus, it is permissible to speculate that the long and grueling American involvement may just possibly have accomplished its purpose, that it did save large areas of Southeast Asia, that it did pave the way for happier relationships between the great powers in the years to come. On the other hand, a number of qualified observers consider the domino theory to be unproved and unprovable nonsense. Historians, as usual, are likely to have the last word.

Whatever the eventual outcome of the American involvement, it is certain that the United States paid a terrible price. Not alone in lives and dollars but in human values: a divided nation, a rising crime rate, a soaring increase in drug addiction, the scrapping on the home front of most of the programs designed to combat poverty and social injustice— all the grave and painful problems which were officially ignored while the war was prosecuted. It can only be hoped that the war bears some sort of acceptable fruit, that somehow there will be value received commensurate with the strenuousness of the effort—although on this matter, as is true of all wars, no one will know the opinion of the dead.

25th Infantry leaves divisional
bolt-of-lightning insignia in civilian
victim's mouth, Quang Ngai Province, 1967.

Above: Hue, 1968.
Right: VC, Saigon, 1968.
Following pages: Suspected VC, 1967.

Above: Shortly before artillery
destroyed this village, this woman,
this child, Quang Ngai Province, 1967.
Right: Victim of helicopter rocket,
Saigon, 1968.

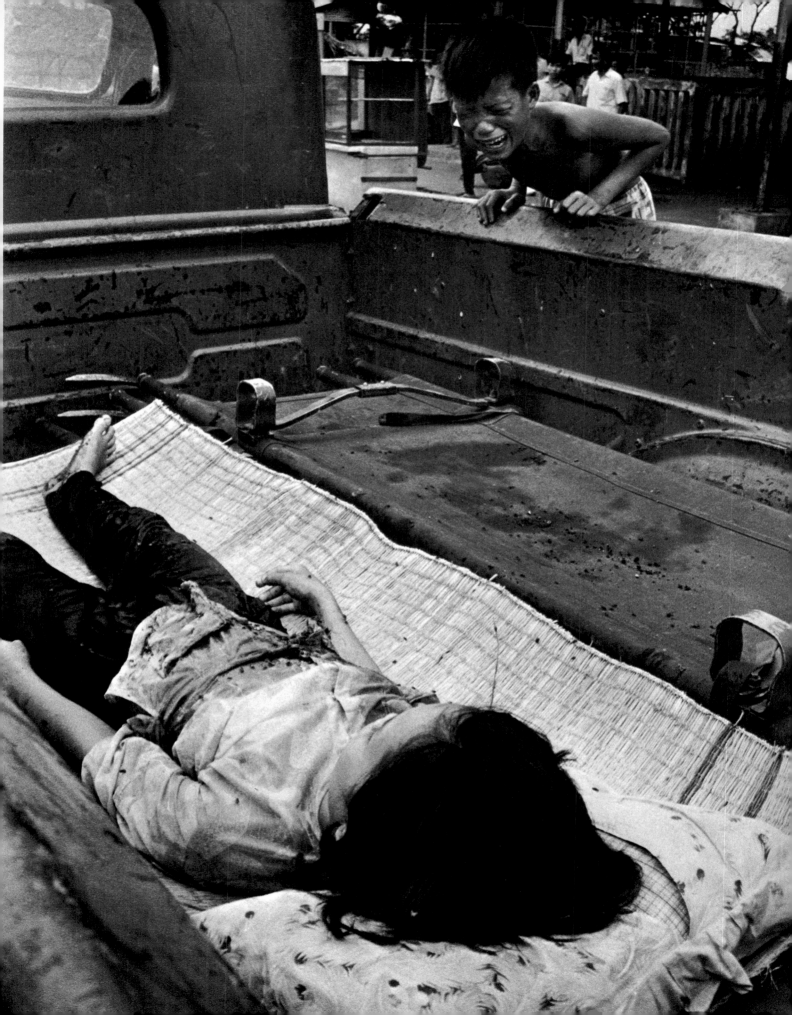

Opposite (from l): Commanding general,
1st ARVN Infantry; commander, 26th Marine
Regiment; commanding general, 1st
Cavalry Division, Khe Sanh, 1968.
Above: Ben Tre, 1968.

238

Bomber catapulted from carrier deck, 1971. Following pages: U.S. Marines, Hue, 1968.

DONALD MCCULLIN—MAGNUM

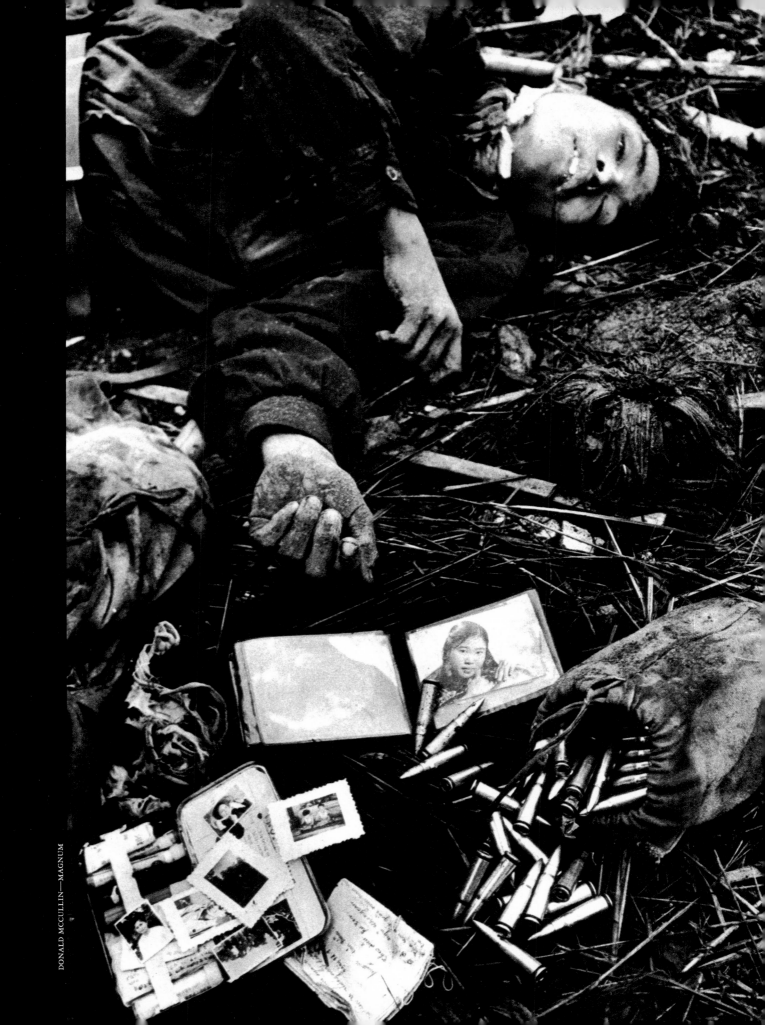

Helicopter taking off with wounded.

ARVN base, Han Ngli, 1971.

U.S. armor, 1971. Following pages: Ashua Valley, 1968.

The Photography of War

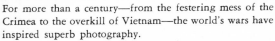

For more than a century—from the festering mess of the Crimea to the overkill of Vietnam—the world's wars have inspired superb photography.

Roger Fenton was the first to cover a war coherently. His stately Victorian views of Britain's Crimean misadventure were the more remarkable for the unwieldiness of his camera and equipment. The requirement that plates be exposed while wet and developed immediately (in the traveling darkroom, above) limited his output to several pictures a day. (By contrast, motorized 35-mm cameras available today can take hundreds of shots in minutes.)

Yet no good photographer has ever been inhibited by his equipment, and between Fenton and the present a host of brave and skillful picture reporters—known and unknown—has recorded the spectacular destruction, the legal violence, and the great pain of war.

The scene at bottom shows a Civil War tent-darkroom of the sort Mathew Brady and Timothy O'Sullivan must have used. At top is a cluster of still and movie cameramen of World War I. In the small picture below is Capt. Edward Steichen, who photographed World War I from early bombers and then commanded the photographic task force that covered the U.S. Navy in World War II. The woman below is Leni Riefenstahl, whose photography was a potent propaganda weapon in persuading the world that Nazi Germany was invincible in the 1930s.

And the single figure with hands in pockets is Robert Capa, the greatest of them all, in whose tradition the best contemporary war photographers follow. He revolutionized the photojournalism of war in Spain, and—fascinated and revulsed—continued to report the wars of his time until, in Vietnam in 1954, war killed him, too.